STRONGER STILL

Other books in the Deeper Still Series

Deeper Still

STRONGER STILL

A Woman's Guide
to Turning Your Hurt into Healing for Others

By Edna Ellison

Birmingham, Alabama

New Hope® Publishers
P. O. Box 12065
Birmingham, AL 35202-2065
www.newhopepublishers.com

Library of Congress Cataloging-in-Publication Data

Ellison, Edna.
  Stronger still : a woman's guide to turning your hurt into healing for others / Edna Ellison.
    p. cm.
  ISBN 978-1-59669-090-5 (sc)
  1. Christian women—Religious life—Textbooks. 2. Church work—Textbooks. 3. Evangelistic work—Textbooks. I. Title.
  BV4527.E463 2007
  248.8'43—dc22
          2007009947

ISBN: 978-1-59669-090-5

N074139 • 0707 • 4M1

DEDICATION

To my ancestors, who experienced the tough times of life long before I did. These faithful grandparents and parents set a godly Christian standard for my family for generations to come: Chesley Mack Watson and Edna Dempsey Poole, Clarence Irvin and Florence Cooper Martin, James Ernest (Deany) and Mary Mack Poole Martin.

ABOUT THE AUTHOR

———————— • ————————

A popular author and speaker, Edna Ellison has enjoyed leading Bible studies, prayer retreats and women's conferences in London, England; Frankfurt, Germany; cities in Panama and Honduras; and in almost every state in America, including Alaska and Hawaii. She has also written articles for *LifeWise*, a Focus on the Family magazine, and the story of her life has been featured in its pages. She has been interviewed on radio and television shows in several states. She enjoys traveling, writing, and meeting new friends.

A native of Clinton, South Carolina, Ellison earned a PhD from the University of Alabama and other degrees from the University of South Carolina, Converse College, and Presbyterian College. She has taught at universities, colleges, and seminaries in America and abroad. She has also served as editor for a national Christian women's magazine (*Royal Service*), and has written for *Missions Mosaic* magazine, and *Christian Single*, as well as others. Called "the Christian mentoring guru," she has written two books on mentoring: *Seeking Wisdom: Preparing Yourself to Be Mentored* (available from ednae9@aol.com), and *Woman to Woman: Preparing Yourself to Mentor* (available from www.newhopepubl.com or your local bookstore). Other books include the *Friend to Friend* Bible study series for two friends to study together: *Friend to Friend: A Shared Study of Philippians, Friendships of Faith: A Shared Study of Hebrews,* and *Friendships of Purpose: A Shared Study of Ephesians* (All available from www.newhopepublishers.com.)

A humorist, Edna also loves collecting Christian jokes and leading women in her church in The Beautiful Hat Society (www.thebeautifulhatsociety.com), a group of Christian women who meet monthly at a different restaurant for lunch, swap jokes, exchange white elephant gifts, and talk about their mentoring adventures. Her favorite topic is "Born to Be the Ultimate Me." To contact Edna Ellison, email her at ednae9@aol.com or find her on her Web site: www.ednaellison.com.

Edna's family calls her "Mimi." She is incredibly proud of her two adult children, Patsy Farmer and Jack Ellison; their spouses, Tim and Wendy; and granddaughter, Blakely.

TABLE OF CONTENTS

———————— • ————————

ACKNOWLEDGMENTS

●
_____   _____

When one writes a book, she owes more than she could ever repay. God enabled a team to prepare this book for publication. I am grateful to the wonderful staff of New Hope Publishers for their tireless work. Its capable president and publisher, Andrea Mullins, gave courageous leadership to the process from the beginning. As a life-long friend, she's an inspiration to me, and she believes in me. What greater thing could one treasure about a dear friend? She's an inspiration to many godly Christian women as she lives an exemplary life of love.

My sincere thanks to Joyce Dinkins, New Hope's managing editor for overseeing this project. Rebecca England, finalist for the Golden Scroll Award from the international Advanced Writers and Speakers Association, deserves accolades for hours of editing. In her sweet, affirming way, she has contributed to the book. Also, assistant editor Ella Robinson has spent many hours proofreading and attending to details to coordinate the words, style, and artwork through their final edit. I am thankful for her competent work as well as her friendly spirit and willingness to accommodate the ideas of the author. In addition, a big thanks goes to Freda Souter, the graphic designer who helped with the project.

As with other books I've written, I owe many thanks to my family, who have stood by me as I've tried out ideas on them, used them as illustrations for my writing, and discussed the tough times of life. We have a joke in my family: none of them remember stories I relate exactly the way I remember them. They have been patient to trust my memory and not complain when I've misquoted them or left out important things they remember.

To Jack: You're the best son any mother ever had. You're patient, kind, and loving, always seeking peace, and trying to make my life and the lives of others around you better. I appreciate your being a loving husband and a good father with just the right touch of discipline and tenderness. I'm proud of your service to God and your faithfulness to your church. I admire your spirit in helping your mother- and father-in-law, Peggy and Bob Prickett; walking their dog, Duncan; mowing their lawn; and doing handyman jobs around the house when they need you. I appreciate your sense of humor, as you entertain us with animated gestures and comic faces. Blakely and I will always remember.

To Patsy: You're the best daughter any mother ever had. You're talented and sweet with a great sense of charm and style in everything you do. Thank you for sharing your home and your life with me every day. What would I do without you to go to Curves with me, cook for me, and shop with me? I appreciate your allowing me to pile up stacks of ideas I call "fodder" and amass baskets of information for the next book. Thank you for remaining patient with me when I forget everything else to finish a chapter on a book. I know you and Jack share my love for Christ, the most joyous part of parenthood, and inspiration for my writing. Since your father died, you have both been my life.

Thank you to the in-laws, Wendy and Tim, for being faithful spouses to my two dear children and for loving your mother-in-law.

I thank God for you often. And special thanks to Blakely, my six-year-old granddaughter, the light of my life. Her "Hello, Mimi! When you comin' to see me?" is the most joyous sound in the world. God has been good to me, blessing me with far more than I deserve: the kind words of two successful Christian children, the good relationships with adult children-in-law, and the sweet hugs and kisses from a darling, beautiful little girl who plays "O Come, Little Children," on the violin. Thank you, God, for giving me inspiration to write for You.

INTRODUCTION:
WHEN THE NIGHT IS DARK

——————————— • ———————————

If you've picked up this book to read it, you may be experiencing a crisis or trial. If you're not facing one now, you can certainly remember past troubles, and expect to face more in the future! How often have you, or I, or any number of people felt they were standing in deep water, almost over their heads?

You may answer, "Nearly every day!" for every human being experiences circumstances that give palpitations of fear or despair. Sometimes you think you can't go on. Today may be the day you're neck-deep in trouble that attacks the deepest part of your heart: your children are ill, your spouse unfaithful, your teenagers rebellious, your sister bitter, your parents dying . . . the list of possibilities goes on. As much as you regret it, your spiritual stamina is waning, unable to sustain you through the crises of life. You find your faith floundering—you may even be questioning the existence of God.

How do you react? Sometimes you paint on a plastic smile,

pretending you don't hurt. Other times, you set your will as firmly as possible: you're determined to attend church regularly, observe daily devotions scrupulously, study your Bible, and pray fervently. Frantic religious activity brings neither spiritual nor physical rest. It may increase your anxiety. There seems to be no end to trouble.

God has the answer; He's the Master of Peace. This book is designed to show how God alleviates pain when the night is dark—before, during, and after a crisis. He promises to unfold His personal message to you as He calls you to follow Christ through all the tough times of your life. Rather than flounder and drown in a "sea of troubles," as Shakespeare said, you can dive deeper into the Spirit of Christ and swim safely to calm shores.

Unit 1

——————— ● ———————

EXPERIENCING THE
PITFALLS OF REAL LIFE

Face it: we don't live in a stable universe. As long as we live on this planet, it will be rushing through space at greater-than-warp speed. The spinning earth is divided into giant plates—each containing vast continents or oceans—that shift beneath our feet, causing earthquakes, floods, and volcanic eruptions. As the earth spins on its axis, our lives also are spinning. Sometimes it makes no sense.

Though we accept that chaotic macrocosm as a scientific fact, we fail to perceive it realistically, because we're too busy with the "cares of this world" (Matthew 13:22 NKJV). Humans have a tradition, corporately and individually, of trying to build a rational world, a solid society with rules everyone obeys. As one who lives on this earth, you've inherited this legacy.

You've also inherited the legacy of the Fall. Since Adam and Eve, you've had ancestors for generations who were sinful from the beginning, as Psalm 51:5 says. As much as possible, you try to live a good life and avoid sin. It's easy to slip into the habits of human social life. You buy land, build a home, collect possessions, and save money as if you believe you'll live forever on earth, but that assumption is unrealistic. You live in a precarious world, which is reflected in your own little microcosm, where you live through one crisis after another.

However, God brings hope to each human heart. He who created the world still orders it. He brings order out of chaos just as He did at Creation. As you read this unit, remember, you're important to God. He's the source of all love, since He is love (1 John 4:16b). He wants to give you His peace, comfort, and the revelation of truth. He created truth for all people, and you can see it through other obedient Christians. If you'd like to be one of those mature, contented, strong Christians, read on:

. . . .

O, Lord of all, why must I hurt?
Why don't I ever understand?
I wonder how You run this world
When it is changing, shifting sand.
 I know you hear me, List'ning Lord.
 I trust it's steady in Your hand.

—ee

. . . .

—— Study 1 ——

Holy Coincidences:
God Is Master

This book focuses on one major premise: God is Master of the universe. He proves His sovereignty continuously in daily life.

Jack and Sharon Fields McCormick are typical Americans who fell in love, married, and moved to a nice neighborhood. Though Sharon and Jack had faith in God—both of them accepting Jesus as their personal Savior—they pursued secular jobs. Jack was in management with a construction company. Sharon finished her master's degree in counseling and worked for a mental health facility. Each earned a more-than-adequate salary. They owned a big brick home on large acreage, two cars and a pickup truck, a pool, a boat, and a motorcycle, along with other luxuries. Soon they bought a motor home, planning extended travels around the country.

While the McCormicks were acquiring expensive possessions, their church was building their faith. They became tithers, and gave extra offerings to special causes, especially missions endeavors. On a "chance" encounter, they heard of a training event for disaster relief in the next county. They drove over to learn about it, perhaps to share with their Sunday School class later. At the training conference, they learned of an urgent need in the US for men knowledgeable in construction and for women who had counseling skills. Volunteers would need a motor home to provide their own lodging. This information pierced their hearts, and it was the beginning of a "holy coincidence."

Sharon and Jack returned, going to church the next Sunday, when their pastor preached a missions sermon. When they left, Jack said, "It was all I could do to keep from running down the aisle to volunteer!" Sharon turned to him. "I held onto the pew in front of me. I wanted to make a commitment to missions too!" She turned aside, then back to face him: "Oh, my goodness; Jack, I think God's calling us to be missionaries!"

They visited the pastor that week. "Tell us what to do," they said.

He laughed. "You want me to tell you what God is saying to you?" he asked. They realized how misdirected their request was, and the next day they announced in front of their congregation they were going to be missionaries. After receiving training, they sold their home (in four days!), furniture, and vehicles and went to War.

War, West Virginia, was the poorest town in the poorest county in Appalachia. Setting up their motor home, they began organizing hundreds of volunteers from all over the US who came to help fight poverty. They learned to depend on God alone for support, since they had gone from two lucrative salaries to none.

Reflecting back, Sharon (sfieldsmccormick@prodigy.net) saw that God had miraculously taught them to trust, to discern God's will for their lives, and to receive power from Him to act on His will.

Have you ever experienced a Holy coincidence? If so, tell what happened: _____

_____

_____

_____

_____

Share your story with a friend.

Twenty Steps to Understanding God as Master

1. God created the universe.
2. If He created it, then He owns it, is sovereign over it—the Master of all.
3. If God is Master of all, then He's Master, not only of all nature, but also of all people.
4. If He's Master of all people, then—since you're a person—He's your personal Master (ruler, director, teacher).
5. If God is your personal, Sovereign Master, He rules over your circumstances and your heart.
6. If He rules your circumstances, then you can trust Him to take care of you.
7. If you trust God to take care of you, you won't worry about anything.
8. If you don't worry, you have God's peace in your heart.
9. If God's peace rules your heart, you know He wants an intimate, personal relationship (See more about this concept in Study 3).
10. If you've invited Him to have a personal relationship with you, He gives you joy, passion for life.
11. If God gives you a passion for certain things in life, then He's filling you with the desire to serve Him.
12. If He fills you with the desire to serve Him, He'll show you how to serve Him.
13. If God shows you how to serve Him, He'll enable, empower, you to do His will.
14. If He empowers you to serve Him, you'll get opportunities of a lifetime: to be a part of God's plan for the world.
15. If you become a part of His plan for the world—and since you were created in His image (Genesis 1:27)—then you will become more like God every day.

16. If you become more like God, He lives within you and you can live in Him—heart (or spirit), soul, and body.
17. If you live in Him, you'll live a Spirit life and approach spiritual maturity.
18. As you approach spiritual maturity, you'll see spiritual occurrences in everyday life.
19. As you see spiritual occurrences, you absorb the will and heart of God.
20. As you absorb the ultimate will and heart of God, you move into heaven, to be with Him.

If you believe God created the world, then all other miracles of God, as His Spirit moves over the face of the earth, are easy to believe. You accept that He's the Sovereign Master of the world you live in. You know He controls all coincidences—and indeed every incident in your life. The word *coincidence* begins with the Latin prefix, co, (joined; working in tandem, as in cooperate, and coordinate). He's the co-pilot of all your incidents—everything you control through your free will: children; work situation; habits; and relationships. As you voluntarily relinquish these to Him, He brings peace, joy, and order to your life.

Look at the 20 steps above. Which one(s) are hardest for you to understand? _____

_____

Write what you might do to understand God better.

_____

_____

_____

Sovereign Master of All Order

Since God brings order to everyday life, you can depend on life to be predictable, right?

Wrong. You, like everyone else, experience the breathlessness of daily surprises. Sometimes you think they're good; sometimes, bad. Christians and others react in two ways to daily events: intuitively or logically.

Some Christians seem able to foresee surprises. If you're an intuitive person, you may expect surprises before they occur because of certain laws of nature, unexplained feelings, or uncanny dreams. You may say you've experienced Murphy's Law; that is, whatever can go wrong, will go wrong. For example, no matter which checkout line you stand in at the grocery store, it's always the longest.

Whether negative or positive, if you're a Christian, you're always alert to discern spiritual matters, looking for miracles—not from chance, astrological signs, or feelings, but from God.

A second way Christians react to the world's unpredictable surprises is with logic. You may have no intuition whatsoever, reacting cognitively, with a logical explanation for every miracle before you. God has to wake you up to spiritual matters, because you ignore them most of the time. Whether you tend to be a spiritually intuitive person or a logical-thinking person, you can't deny there's more to life than the physical universe. God speaks to us in many ways.

God's Ever-Present Presence

Nature: How could anyone deny that an intelligent designer created the universe? God produced multicolored flowers to bloom spontaneously on remote mountainsides and in dry deserts. God says, "The mountains and hills will burst into song before you, and all the trees of the field will clap their hands" (Isaiah 55:12). All nature is a manifestation of His handiwork.

Music: God has given the world a special touch of music, which has "charms to soothe the savage beast" within us. Ronnie King, my cousin, once told me he hardly remembered what the pastor said in a sermon, but he was always touched by the music. His words impressed me because I'd rarely been moved by music but love thought-provoking sermons. God has provided both to reach us with His message (Psalm 150).

The Word: John states it succinctly: "In the beginning was the Word, and the Word was with God, and the Word was God" (John 1:1). John, of course, is describing the Logos, Greek for "word"; but in addition to the Scriptures God gave us, he refers to the Logos as Jesus, who was present at Creation and later was incarnate in the first century.

You often hear Christians say God's Word comes alive as they read the Bible. Perhaps you've had the experience of reading Scripture randomly, and then one line stands out, calling your attention. It speaks to your heart at its deepest level.

Other Humans: Sometimes God speaks through sermons, discussions, radio programs, or a short phrase spoken by a godly Christian friend in a passing moment. You may not be paying attention, but suddenly the spoken word comes alive in others' words. You recognize it as God, not them.

Direct Revelation: During moments of meditation, sometimes God impresses on you a certain phrase or sentence that passes through your mind, persisting until you notice it. You realize God is revealing His plan: something you can do, say, or pray as you fulfill His will for your life.

Circumstances: The most astounding way God can work to surprise you with His presence is through changing circumstances in your days.

You get a hint of God's sovereignty as you experience what I call "holy coincidences"; *that is, something happens that seems purely coincidence, yet you later realize God was working out a holy moment in His will for your life.* You may say, "It was a God thing." Many Christians like the McCormicks can give you examples of these holy coincidences: a flat tire leads to a witness at the tire shop, an accident leads doctors to discover and prevent a more serious physical problem, or a disaster turns out to be the best blessing of your life! Oswald Chambers calls these "parentheses." (See more about parentheses, or holy coincidences in Study 14). He says God interrupts your busy day with a parenthesis, and then you move on; but afterwards, you may never be the same!

M & M: Ministry and Missions Moment

Do you believe the 20 steps to understanding God as Master? Whether you tend to be intuitive or logical, God finds unique ways to reach you. He reveals, step by step, His presence in your life. However you perceive Him, accept His will—let His love flow out—though a holy moment this week.

——— Study 2 ———

Hope in the Future: God Is Lord

One summer afternoon, while Daddy was at work and Mother was at home with my brother Jim and me, the sky became dark. "A storm's coming," Mother said. "Maybe we'll get some rain for the flowers."

"Since we can't play outside, let's bake cookies," Jim said. As it began raining, Mother mixed butter with dry ingredients and milk, and then let us help beat the batter. "I need a teaspoon of vanilla flavoring," she said. "I'm going next door. Want to go?"

Quickly we got underneath Mother's umbrella and made the short trip to the next house. When Mother knocked on the door, no one answered. She knew Mrs. Gayner was at home, so she called. I could hear my friend, Annie, so I called, "Annie! It's me. Edna!"

In a minute Annie came to the door. We found her mother and brother behind the sofa! All three had been hiding from the storm. I'll never forget Mother's remarks on the way home: "Mrs. Gayner must not be a Christian. Christians are never afraid. In case of rain, we carry umbrellas and use the common sense God gives us, but then we trust Him to take care of us."

From the time I was a little girl, I knew God would take care of us no matter what happened. Mother gave her children a good example of a mature, trusting Christian. She believed in a personal

God who wanted relationship with her and all His children. We grew up knowing God was Master of the rainstorms and sunshine, Creator of the universe, yet the personal God of a yielding heart, always asking to come in. When I was a preteen, I invited Jesus into my heart to become, not my mother's Lord, but the personal Lord of my life. From that moment on, God began teaching me His will for my life. My experience is nothing unusual among Christians. Bit by bit, as troubles and challenges come, He encourages you to give everything to Him. As you walk the sacrificial pathway, troubles common to all humankind push you closer to God. As a Christ follower, you learn step by step, to give everything you are and have to Him.

The Mystery of a Follower's Life

Mark recalls a day in Jesus's life that gives us insight into the mysterious sacrificial life of His followers. As disciples followed Jesus to Jerusalem (Mark 10:32), a rich young ruler approached Jesus. Jesus told the young man that his scrupulous following of the law was not the way to heaven. It's impossible to earn your way into the presence of God. Since Jesus saw the man's greedy heart, He diagnosed his dependence on material things, telling him he could be saved by selling everything he had and giving it to the poor. When the young man went away sorrowful, Jesus told His disciples, "It is easier for a camel to go through the eye of a needle than for a rich man to enter the kingdom of God" (Mark 10:24). In Jesus's day, of course, next to every wide gate in the walls of most cities was a small pedestrian gate called the "eye of a needle," which was very low, allowing no chariots, carts, or animals to go through. After the large gate had been shut for security at night, if a man riding a camel decided to enter, he had to place his camel on its knees and push it through. Since camels are stubborn creatures, it may have taken hours to coax and beat a camel to get it inside an eye-of-a-needle gate. In the first century, camels being pushed through after dark was not unusual, but it always caused an uproar. The common people would have recognized Jesus's allusion: it was extremely difficult (but not impossible) for a camel to go through the eye of a needle. Because wealthy people depend on their money/influence, it's hard to depend on Christ alone for all sustenance—physical and spiritual.

Someone has said the poorest person in America today is richer than the richest person in Jesus's day. If that statement is true, with which of the characters in this story do you relate?
a. **The rich young ruler, since I own many possessions, with money in the bank, assets, and investments.**
b. **The chief priests, since I'm a well-respected member of my church.**
c. **The teachers of the law, since I'm a Bible study teacher, and/or a volunteer or paid church staff.**
d. **One of the disciples, since I understand I can't earn my way to heaven by being good.**
e. **Jesus, since I know that no one is good except God Himself. I believe things impossible for humans are possible with God (Mark 10:27).**
f. **Several of these characters, since I recognize myself in several of their traits.**

Jesus said, "Follow me" (Mark 10:21). Have you left something to follow Jesus? Explain.

_____

_____

_____

_____

Read Mark 1:16–18. Summarize Simon Peter's and Andrew's call and response.

_____

_____

_____

Hearing the Call

Peter said, "We have left everything to follow you" (Mark 10:28). Simon Peter and his brother Andrew were fishing in the Sea of Galilee when Jesus called, "Come, follow me" (Mark 1:16-18). Mark recounts: "At once they left their nets and followed him." They offer an ideal response to God's call. Stop, drop, and walk. (Stop what you're doing; drop everything; and walk toward Christ.) First you acknowledge Him as Sovereign Master of the universe (Study 1), accept Him as the Lord of your life (Study 2). Then, as you move deeper in His heart (See below), you begin to focus on His call.

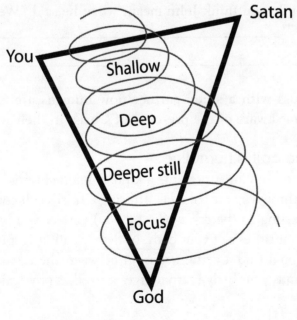

1. The call is amazing.

Mark uses the phrase, "the disciples were amazed" several times in his account of the march toward Jerusalem (Mark 10:24, 26, 32). Not just the 12 disciples, but all the true Christ-followers felt the amazing call: "the whole crowd was amazed" (Mark 11:18). Imagine what the crowd might have felt if they realized that Almighty God had come to dwell among them (John 1:14). Of all the world religions, it is truly amazing that *Christianity is the only one in which God Himself lived as a man and died for the sins of all humanity.* As you stand in fear and amazement, your first reaction to the call is to praise Him.

Read John 1:14. What's your personal reaction to these words: "The Word [Logos, or Jesus]. . . made his dwelling among us"? Explain.

_____

_____

What do you think John meant when he said "We have seen his glory"?_____

_____

Discuss with a study partner how humans are amazed as they become aware of the presence of Christ in their lives.

2. The call is humbling.

The call of Christ presents a kind of *spiritual vertigo*, which at first may throw you off-balance. Trusting Christ's call completely is disconcerting to the *carnal* (flesh/body) part of you because His call is the antithesis of your body, or fleshly call; it is spiritual. All your life you'll find a certain tension between these two. This tension demands your body (carnal urges as well as physical stature) be set aside in favor of the Spirit (the Holy Spirit which dwells in you). [See more about this tension in upcoming chapters]. On this subject, Jesus gave a good answer to James and John, when they asked to have seats on Jesus's right and left—second and third in command in the kingdom of God. Our Lord, thinking of the humbling suffering of a Christian's ego, or *self*, as he or she becomes stronger in the *spiritual* things of life, said, "You don't know what you are asking" (Mark 10:38). "Whoever wants to become great among you must be your servant. And whoever wants to be first must be slave of all" (Mark 10:43-44). Shortly before, He'd said, "But many who are the first will be last, and the last shall be first." Paul said later: "In humility consider others better than yourselves" (Philippians 2:3).

The call of God for every Christian is one of lowliness, unselfishness, and heart-core humility.

3. The call is an experience of trust.
An old-but-good definition of faith is Forsaking All, I Trust Him. As a Christian, you take the leap of faith, into the arms of Jesus. You trust the Holy Spirit—even if you're in troubled waters: through shallow/meager living, good/bad income, disappointment in others/God, in sickness/health, and even through the valley of the shadow of death (Psalm 23:4). It takes courage to be a Christian because you must face *abandonment of self and love God at all costs.* Job said, "Though he slay me, yet will I hope in him" (Job 13:15).

M & M: *Ministry and Missions Moment*
Are you willing to trust Him to care for your family, job, church, friends, and all personal needs? This week, relinquish your control, putting faith in Him, period. As a mature Christian, tell Him you're willing to lose all in service for Him—even when He asks you to do hard or impossible things.

Study 3

Make the Sacrifice: God Is Fellow Laborer

Linda Goldstein is the aunt of Scott Quarles, a Christian young man and poet who was killed on duty as a county deputy sheriff in June 2003. Linda says, "At 2:00 A.M. I got a call about the horrible tragedy. My 22 years as an ER nurse didn't prepare me for the shock that night. My husband, Lee, and our youngest son, Jamie, were in Haiti on a medical mission trip at the time, but God took care of us through the night and the weeks that followed." Linda admires her sister Margaret, Scott's mother and also a nurse, who showed great spiritual strength and used her tragic experience to help others.

In 2005, Linda and Lee went to Charleston for the wedding of a close friend's daughter. After the wedding, they sat and talked with a friend, Beth, and her friend, Katy. Linda says, "Katy and I hit it off right away. She told of having cancer 25 years ago and being blessed with twin daughters who were now 21. Somehow the subject of Scott came up, and we talked about his death and how God had taken care of us. Katy said, 'How do you ever prepare yourself for something like that? I cannot imagine.' When Lee and I went to watch the bride and groom cut the cake, the minister's wife came over and said, 'Your friend needs you.'

"Katy had just gotten a call from her husband that one of her twins, Whitney, had drowned at Baker's Creek State Park. What a God moment!

"I thought, first with panic, then with confidence, 'I've been here before. I've done this.' Then I realized I was there for a reason. Lee and I prayed with them, went to their hotel, and helped them pack and get on the road—calling several times later. I've thought about that conversation with Katy and the events that followed, and somehow, in our loss of Scott, being able to help someone else has been comforting for me."

Fellow Laborers with God

Linda was in yoke with God as she ministered to Katy. Paul says, "For we are God's fellow workers" (1 Corinthians 3:9 NKJV). God wants us in yoke with Him. Scholars debate whether this Scripture means all of us are *yoked together with fellow laborers* that follow God, or whether we're *yoked with* God as an integral part of the gospel's work on earth. Either way, we're servants of God, yoked together in the awesome job of sharing His witness on earth. Because Linda had "been there/done that," she was uniquely qualified to give Katy hope in her hour of need. God arranged for Linda to be His spokes-person-comforter in that crisis.

God expects us:
1. To be in harness with Christ—even in troubled times.
2. To be submissive, not resisting the yoke.
3. To believe the burdens of life are easier through Him.
4. To have hope for the future and joy in spite of tragedy.

Have you ever been in a unique position as Linda was at the wedding?_____ Share your story with a study partner.

How easy is it for you to be submissive to the yoke of a Christian worker (number 2 above)?

_____

_____

Do you honestly believe the burdens of life are easier through Him (number 3 above)? Why or why not?

_____

_____

When did you find hope in spite of a tragedy? Explain.

_____

_____

Christians' Major Mistake

One major mistake of today's Christians is that they expect everything in life to work out well if they become Christians. They have a Pollyanna outlook on life. Some of them even see the cross as a charm that they can wear around their necks for good luck.

The Call Is Frightening

On the contrary, allowing yourself to be yoked with Christ is an astounding thought, requiring a trust that makes you hesitate with fear. Look back at Mark 10:28–32. Mark says the disciples were astonished, while others who followed were afraid. C. S. Lewis says one of the objections to Christianity is that the cross is offensive. He says the cross is offensive even to him—a Christian—and probably is to most Christians. It is a bloody, horrible symbol, which few can embrace. I dare say Jesus Himself found it offensive. The last week of Jesus's life, He and the disciples were headed toward

Jerusalem. He knew the fearsome, offensive death He faced, yet He walked steadily toward it. Later we see His human feelings as He prayed in Gethsemane for God to take "the cup"—His offensive, horrible death on the cross—away from Him.

Mature Christians fear God, but they aren't *afraid of Him*. How can that be? They approach Him with honest reverence and respect for who He is. God says, "The fear of the Lord is the beginning of wisdom" (Proverbs. 9:10). Christians aren't afraid of Him or the future because they respect and trust Him. After all, Jesus lived as a man and died to "free those who all their lives were held in slavery by their fear of death" (Hebrews 2:15). We neither fear death nor the Almighty Judge because we know He's a God of love. In fact, He *IS* love (1 John 4:16).

The Call Is Self-Sacrificing

If Christ invites you to be yoked with Him as a fellow laborer, you realistically face a sacrifice.

The disciples and other Jews expected the Messiah to be a secular Jewish king with political power. No wonder they were astonished when Jesus warned them of impending sacrifices! He mentioned leaving their homes, parents, siblings, and children; they would sacrifice their "fields," or businesses (Mark 10:29), and suffer persecution for their faith. As predicted, Christians were later tortured, flogged, imprisoned, stoned, sawed in two, and forced to live in caves (Hebrews 11:35*b*-38).

When those who followed Him that day heard these warnings, I imagine it was hard for them to accept their call to suffering and self-sacrifice. They didn't understand the call to suffer as Paul did, who later said: "I consider everything a loss compared to the surpassing greatness of knowing Christ Jesus my Lord, for whose sake I have lost all things. I consider them rubbish, that I may gain Christ and be found in him . . . I want to know . . . the fellowship of sharing in his sufferings, becoming like Him in His death, and so, somehow, to attain to the resurrection from the dead" (Philippians 3:8-11). Again we see the tension in the Christian life: *Lose all things; gain Christ. Reject the world; be found in Him. Know Him; share in His sufferings. Be like Him in death; attain resurrection.*

Read Philippians 3:9. What important concept has been omitted in the quote above (verses 8, 10–11)? Write its meaning.

_____

_____

_____

What are the two requirements of true righteousness?

_____

_____

What's the difference between "righteousness of my own that comes from the law" and true righteousness?

_____

_____

How does *giving up your own righteousness,* that is, *depending on self-righteous moral rules* serve as an avenue to self-sacrifice? Explain with examples from your own life.

_____

_____

The Call Is Often Followed by Evil Attack

Some in the crowd who were afraid of Jesus were the chief priests and the teachers of the law. Mark says they feared Him because the crowd was amazed at His teaching, and they plotted to kill Him (Mark 11:18).

How many new Christians have you seen come under attack when they decide to follow Jesus? This is a principle of your discipleship call: *the closer you grow to Christ, the more opposition you can expect from Satan.* (Check the proximity in Figure 1, found in Study 2.) Often just after you've turned over a new leaf, deciding to live for Christ, you experience attack. If the evil one cannot attack you through temptation (to lust/ covet/ smear your personality) he will attack through nature (loved one's death/ accident/ sickness/ breakup of a relationship). God allows these attacks only in His permissive will. He's never the author of sadness and chaos. As a maturing Christian following your Lord's call, you'll recognize these things for what they are: outright evil attack. In fact, if you're not experiencing the tensions of opposition, you might need to question your obedience to God's call.

The Call Is Painful

A yoke chafes a young ox's skin. You may find your spiritual yoke, willingly taken, mutually acceptable to laborers, causes pain. You draw away from the pain of being yoked as a fellow-laborer with Christ.

Watchman Nee says your soul must be cracked open like a seed-pod, to get to the inner layer, where life is. You must be stripped of everything *you* to become everything *Him.* God, the Master Potter, shapes you, molds you as a fit vessel for His love. He continues to peel layers of shallowness to open your heart core to His truth.

As you realize, no change is easy. The process brings pain, as you become vulnerable. As humans, we cling to the comfort of our humanity: money, sex, time, possessions, anger, and revenge. We feel better about ourselves if we're better than the Joneses; we elevate ourselves by putting others down. To set aside favorite off-color television shows; Web sites bordering on pornography; and the cigarettes, drinks, or drugs that numb you from hurt is hard. When God calls you to follow Him, *don't expect a cakewalk. It hurts to deny self.*

The Call Is a Call to Death

"They were on the way up to Jerusalem, with Jesus leading the way" (Mark 10:32). Jesus walked with a purpose, knowing He was going to die shortly. He drew the disciples aside and told them (Mark 10:33–34). "For even the Son of Man did not come to be served, but to serve, and to give his life as a ransom for many" (Mark 10:45). He'd explained death many times before, but it was hard for them to understand their call to follow Him was a call to death. He'd said:

> *"If you obey my commands, you will remain in my love, just as I have obeyed my Father's commands and remain in his love. I have told you this so that my joy may be in you and that your joy may be complete. My command is this: Love each other as I have loved you. Greater love has no one than this, that he lay down his life for his friends. You are my friends if you do what I command. I no longer call you servants, because a servant does not know his master's business. Instead, I have called you friends, for everything that I learned from my Father I have made known to you" (John 15:10-15).*

These are awesome words. God calls you friend because He's disclosed the *secrets of the cross* to you. He says, "If anyone would come after me, he must deny himself and take up his cross daily and follow me" (Luke 9:23).

Dietrich Bonhoeffer was a perfect example of this holy call from Christ. Though his friends helped him escape twice from Nazi Germany during World War II, he returned because he felt compelled to be with God's people, to "console God" Himself when God's own people suffered in concentration camps and gas chambers. Bonhoeffer, who said "When Christ calls a man, He bids him come and die," was hanged outside a concentration camp before the end of the war. G. K. A. Bell, the Anglican Bishop of Chichester, England, said, "Bonhoeffer was a martyr many times before he died." Chichester understood the bit-by-bit, step-by-step, sacrificial life, daily committing more and more self to Christ, submitting area by area of the personal heart to Jesus, the Lord of all. Bonhoeffer had done it: he'd given one area of his heart to God; martyred another bit of self; daily sacrificed self until he understood and lived in the heart and mind of God. (We'll study more about this idea, called "in-living" in Study 9.)

Read Hebrews 12:2–3 and circle the best answer to the following questions.
1. As Christians, we should keep our eyes on
   a) constant alert, to remain righteous.
   b) our business, so we can give church offerings.
   c) Jesus, the author (creator/composer/completer)
      of our faith.
   e) worldly possessions, to supply Christian facilities.

2. Jesus is the author and perfecter (or finisher) of our faith because
   a) He's the only one who can give faith.
   b) His Holy Spirit gives us wisdom to respond in faith.
   c) He's the way to faith: "I am the Way, the Truth, and the Life."

d) His resurrection set the example of our faith in heaven.
e) all the above.

3. Jesus endured the cross
   a) because people killed Him against His will.
   b) because He was ashamed of His suffering.
   c) for the joy set before Him.
   d) so He could sit down at the right hand of God.
   e) so we could become weary and lose heart.

How would you define "the joy set before Him"? Explain.

_____

_____

Discuss your answers with a study friend.

The Joy Is for You Too

Jesus led the way to Jerusalem, just as He leads the way of sacrifice as an example for us. As His "friend" (John 15:15), or disciple, you hear His call to deny *yourself*, take up your cross, and follow Him. Horrible? Not if you have the joy He had as He died for you. Notice the questions above and consider this principle: Jesus endured the cross *for the joy set before Him*. Because He fulfilled God's task for Him, Jesus made it possible for His joy to be in us as well.

M & M: *Ministry and Missions Moment*

Just think of it: you can have Jesus's joy in you. "I have told you this so that my joy may be in *you* . . ." (John 15:11). He loves you so much that He went to the cross willingly to give you eternal life. Your eternity in heaven brings Him joy! Tell others this week about His joy. Celebrate!

——— Study 4 ———

Mysteries into Victories: God Is Revealer

Most of the irony in Western literature is the sad contradiction of situations characters *believe* are true, but aren't really true. The tragedy of Romeo and Juliet is that Romeo killed himself when he found Juliet dead, and then after he died, she woke up from her drugged condition and found *him* dead. In life you sometimes think the worst and the circumstance is actually the best, or vice versa. A young pastoral intern at our church, Derrick Smith, gave this quote: "Most churches are filled with two kinds of members: the righteous who think they're sinners, and sinners who think they're righteous." The secular saying, "perception is reality" is often true, even in a Christian's life.

Human beings—including you and me—are masters at fooling ourselves. We grow up with a self-image that's unrealistic. Entrepreneurs build giant theme parks (one called "the happiest place on earth") to continue the unrealistic experience on earth. We dream of being winners at the top of the pile, thinking more of everything will make us happy. Women hope to be Cinderella: having a beautiful face without nutritious eating; fabulous clothes without working and paying for them; and a gorgeous, rich husband who seeks us wherever we are. We go to seminars to learn how to set goals (such as ten-year plans, and twelve-step programs to rehabilitate our dysfunctional behavior) to improve our lives. We even create a false society to bring order out of our chaos. We form sociological groups to take the place of God's relationship in our lives. We live in planned neighborhoods, with schedules to follow carefully and items to check on our to-do lists. We organize economic systems, such as the American stock market, by buying and selling pork bellies that don't exist and/or earning money by promising not to plant the nonexistent crops on lands we own. We run huge companies by paper frameworks and flow charts that don't exist in real life.

Have you ever fooled yourself? Explain.

_____

_____

Have you ever told a story (a falsehood or an embellishment) until you actually believed it yourself? Explain.

_____

_____

Have you ever had an unrealistic fantasy that seemed realistic? Explain.

_____

_____

Circle the letter below that defines the things you explained above.
a. Unexplained phenomena.
b. Normal activities for all people.
c. Delusions of grandeur.
d. Bouts of neurotic or psychotic thoughts and behavior.
e. Things that happen to other people, but not me.

The Mystery of Mortality

Plato said because of our mortality (temporal, fleshly, carnal bodies), we're creatures chained to the bottom of a cave. Our only recognition of life comes through our five senses—seeing, feeling, hearing, touching, tasting. The senses aren't adequate to allow us to see the entire truth of life's existence, which is outside the cave. According to Plato, there is Light and Truth in an upper world that exists just out of our sight. This light, which is behind us, casts shadows on the cave wall in front of us. We can see light and truth only as we try to discern the shadows of reality on the wall. At some points, a bonfire is lit behind us in an attempt to show a clearer shadow of true models of everything in life that passes between us and the light behind us. At these points we get a glimpse of reality and are able to comprehend the meaning of life. We can learn as we watch carefully everything we see in the shadows. Based on what we discern through our senses, we can devise theories and test them see if they hold true. If they do, we make these theories into scientific laws of nature that govern our world and our behavior.

However, much of all light we receive is not physical, and can't be proven by science. It comes from Christ, who is the Light of the World (John 8:12) and the Spirit of Truth (John 16:13). Our natures have three dimensions: (1) body—physical life; (2) soul—mental, or cognitive, and emotional, or affective life, including our wills; and (3) spirit—our innermost spiritual life, which you may call "soul." In our inner spirits lies the part of us that relates to God. Deep within, that part of us that's born in the image of God relates to Him, yearning to become one with His Spirit (See Study 9). You've probably heard the saying, "You're born with a God-shaped hole in your heart, which only God's Spirit can fill."

The Mystery of our Image

The psalmist talks to God about the inner spirit: "You created my inmost being; you knit me together in my mother's womb" (Psalm 139:13). God created within your inner spirit "His own image, in the image of God" (Genesis 1:27). A mysterious mirror image of God is within you! Your spirit is most comfortable and complete when it has His Spirit within. It fits the hole exactly.

Facing the Truth

An atheist in Liverpool once told me, "Church members are delusional; they don't face the truth." I agree with her to an extent: some church members are clever people with great self-esteem. Some have vacillating emotions, awe-inspiring eloquence, or brilliant intelligence—all of which can fool the person who owns those character traits. Sometimes they depend on themselves because they're self-sufficient; they fail to recognize God's hand in every moment of life.

I remember a time when I didn't face the truth in my own life. I was on a trip in a foreign country with my pastor, his wife, mother-in-law, and other strong Christians when a riot broke out. From our bus windows, we watched small buildings being overturned, people struck with large sticks, and police running after the rioters. Our bus wandered through the volatile area, was blocked by ambulances, and finally escaped down a side street. During the whole episode, the members of our group remained calm. We were disturbed about what has happening to those outside, and wished we could help, but few of us were afraid. Somehow, when God is in charge, Christians don't see through the eyes of the world. We see spiritual light others can't see. We get a glimpse of heaven and eternal outcomes; therefore, we don't see danger as a pragmatic atheist would tell us we should. She might consider us foolish (1 Corinthians 1:23).

Making Sense of Life Through Time

In the middle of the twentieth century, Albert Einstein discovered the theory of relativity, which—among other things—hinted that our ideas about time are misguided, that time is relative. In other words, time is not segmented, as we've artificially implemented it, into days, hours, minutes, and seconds. Age, scientists say, is not caused by time. The centrifugal force of the earth turning (gravity) pulls us down, causing wrinkles and other signs of "aging;" according to the scientists, this is not time. Time is a fallacy. It doesn't exist. We live in a world that we don't understand.

What makes a day? You may quickly answer, "the earth turning one complete revolution on its axis." That's 24 hours, which we divide into two 12-hour segments: A.M. and P.M. Then each of these hours are divided into 60 minutes, which each have 60 seconds, and so on. We rush to meet our goals for every minute. I once worked for an efficiency expert who asked employees to fill out a chart for accomplishments in 15-minute time slots for the 8 hours they worked. We filled each of them with chores we'd done. No one wrote "wasted time," or "talked to a co-worker about nothing important" in any of those slots!

Even those who don't have a job, living in relative leisure, rush to creative writing classes, ball games, or violin lessons. We're bound by segments of time, for work or pleasure. We think what we do is important.

Read this poem and answer the questions below.

> If you can fill the unforgiving minute
> With sixty seconds' worth of distance run,
> Yours is the world and all that's in it—
> And what is more, you'll be a man, my son.
> —*Rudyard Kipling*

1. Why is a minute "unforgiving"?

   _____

2. Are you ever rushed, trying to arrive somewhere or finish a task on time? Give an example.

   _____

   _____

3. How would you define "sixty-seconds' worth of distance run"?

   _____

   _____

4. Explain in your own words: "Yours is the world and all that's in it."

   _____

   _____

5. What kind of maturity is suggested in the last line?

   _____

   _____

6. Overall, what's the message of these lines? Do you agree or disagree?

   _____

   _____

   _____

All your life, you've been taught to live by the clock, an artificial manifestation of time. You've been told the minute is unforgiving, that time well spent flies by— "Time flies when you're having fun"—yet boring, idle time drags slowly. Kipling's poem insinuates that time is important. That you're running a race to do as many good things as possible in your lifetime. That your reward is all the riches, possessions, and success the world has to offer. That you'll be complete, a wise adult, when you achieve these worldly goals.

Time Is Not Real

A. W. Tozer and C. S. Lewis, among others, say that time is a false assumption and an absurdity. We often think God started at point A. At point B, He created the world. At point D, He created humans; at point G, Moses led the exodus; at point L, Jesus was born; at point R, He will return; at point T all Christians will be in heaven; and at point Z, comes the end of "eternity," or infinity. It's hard for you or me to conceive of life without linear history, marked in spots of time.

After each of the following lines, write your opinion.
God is always previous.

_____

_____

_____

Therefore, you can't think of new ways to serve Him or relate to Him that He hasn't already considered.

_____

_____

_____

_____

Therefore, whatever you give to God is reciprocal.

_____

_____

_____

Therefore, whatever _pride_ you have in your own brilliance, originality, love, and ministry is ridiculous.

_____

_____

_____

_____

God the Revealer

Because of your warped view of time and your limited ability to see the truth, as philosophers have tried to explain, you have an unrealistic view of life. Only God can change your view and give you discernment. Through Jesus, God reached down through the heavens, transcending time and space, and gave His only Son to die for you. Life is wrong without Him. Warren Wiersbe says, "Everything is wrong until God sets it right." This is a personal word, spoken just to you. Like the dry bones in the Valley of Death that the prophet Ezekiel saw (Ezekiel 37), you are dead until God breathes life into you. When you recognize your lack of brilliance, originality, love, and ministry, you reciprocate by humbly accepting Jesus Christ as your Savior. Then you come alive, as Jesus draws you near.

His impulse courses within you. As you move deeper and deeper still into the awesome mind and Spirit of the Almighty, He begins to reveal truth. God the Great Revealer clears up the mysteries. He moves you from near-sighted victim to everlasting victor!

Jesus said, "No one can come to me unless the Father who sent me draws him, and I will raise him up at the last day. It is written in the Prophets: 'They will all be taught by God.'. . . I tell you the truth, he who believes has everlasting life" (John 6:43–47).

M & M: Ministry and Missions Moment

There's more at work in your life than meets the eye. God is at the center of all "holy coincidences." Truth hovers just beneath the surface of your everyday life. *When you know who Jesus is, truth is at the center of your spirit!* Growing in Him, learn something this week on the path to knowledge beyond your wildest dreams.

──── Study 5 ────

Champions of the Way: God Is Joy-Giver

I know several wonderful women who are champions of the Way. They know who Jesus is. They're willing to follow Him anywhere because they trust Him, no matter what. They don't blame Him for tragedy in their lives. If He calls them to hardship and sacrifice as they walk the way of the cross, they accept that as an opportunity to witness to His goodness in troubled times.

Joy in Troubled Times

Evelyn Williams is a missions-hearted woman in Mississippi who has great faith through suffering. She says, "Years ago I read that one out of five people would have cancer. I looked at my cancer-free family—4 brothers, 2 parents, 2 children, and 12 nieces and nephews—and wondered if it would ever touch us. In January 1979, I traveled from Clark College, where I worked, to a meeting on the Mississippi coast. While there, I got a call about my youngest brother, Roger, having surgery the next day because of a 'suspicious' kidney. I left the conference immediately to encourage him; his wife; and three daughters, ages 5, 7, and 12. He had a malignancy in the kidney and lymph nodes. After treatment, five years in remission passed until doctors discovered he had brain and chest cancer. Though he had surgery, it was not totally successful.

"Before he died, Roger asked me to call our entire family. I had to call one nephew from a bar, where he says he had 'disregarded his life.' My brother talked with each of them, not to say good-bye, but to ask about their relationship with the Lord. He talked with his older daughter, asking her to live for Christ in such a way that her two younger sisters would want to be Christians. He said to me, 'Evelyn, I know you're a Christian, but I want you to tell me you are.' I told him I was a Christian, and then how special he was, and he replied, 'No, I'm not special. Jesus had to die to save me from my sins.' He talked to all the family, being straightforward in confronting those who didn't live as Christians. Shortly after those phone calls, Roger went to be with the Lord. After he died, his oldest daughter and the nephew found in the bar accepted Christ as their Savior and joined a church. The nephew, who had been having marital troubles, put his marriage back together. Our Lord works in ways that are so awesome!"

Within a short period, Evelyn lost her other brother to cancer and her father from a triple-bypass surgery. After her mother died the same month, Evelyn remarked that things couldn't get worse. She was wrong.

A routine mammogram showed a lump later diagnosed as malignant. She prayed with doctors, family members, groups of prayer warriors, and one special woman who helped her make a decision to have a lumpectomy instead of a complete mastectomy. Suddenly a peace came over her that has remained until today. Though Evelyn had some setbacks during radiation and chemo-therapy, she sees wonderful blessings during those troubled times. She's now been cancer-free for eight years. She points to the Bible, saying, "James says, 'My brethren, count it all joy when you fall into various trials, knowing that the testing of your faith produces patience' (James 1:2 NKJV). I can count it all joy because of how the Lord has walked with me in the path of my journey. I daily seek Him, and He reminds me that each of us is a sinful person and He had to die to save me from my sins. Sin is like cancer; it can come over us so much that it will control us. We have to ask the Lord to forgive us and make us free from sin. So when cancer tries to control our bodies, we must do everything we can: pray; get treatment; and contribute to organizations like Relay for Life and the American Cancer Society that combat this disease. I am grateful to the Lord for organizations like these, for answered prayer, and for life itself, one day at a time."

Joy When Facing Tragedy

Karen Todd, from Greenwood, South Carolina, says, "In 1991, I'd been a wife of a good Christian man, Stacey, for nine years; and the mother of three beautiful children. I loved my family; however, we had drifted from the church and from each other. My husband often played golf five or six days a week until after dark while I stayed home with our children. I had attended church by myself until finally I, too, drifted from church. Not only my husband but also I had let something get between us and God.

"On Friday, November 29, my 8-year-old son, William, begged to go with his grandfather (Papa) bird hunting overnight. Though he'd gone many times in the past, I felt uneasy, as if the Holy Spirit were talking with me. My husband, too, didn't feel at ease with his hunting with Papa. However, after much begging, we let William go.

"I woke up the next morning with that same uneasy feeling I couldn't shake. Usually I went to my Saturday ceramics class, but that day I stayed with my twin girls and then went to my mother's home while Stacey went to play golf as usual.

"About 3:00 P.M., the phone rang. My mother-in-law, Mrs. Todd, was very upset, repeating, 'William has been hurt; you need to go to the hospital." I asked how he was, but she couldn't tell me. I didn't know the number for the golf course, but miraculously, I called it instantly! Finding Stacey in the clubhouse, I told him what was going on. As my father drove me to the hospital, I prayed the whole time, asking God to spare William, to make him well. Not knowing if he were alive was the most horrible feeling I've ever experienced. I was shaking so badly in the car that I later noticed bruises on my leg from repeatedly hitting the door handle.

"Arriving at the hospital, I asked Mrs. Todd what happened. She told me William had been shot. I felt my heart stop. Tears began to flow and the prayers began all over again. About that time, Papa's truck came into the parking lot with my son sitting up in the passenger's seat. I ran to him and grabbed him out of the truck. He had one pellet in the neck and one penetrating his right eye, lodging in his sinus cavity.

"William's damaged right eye required 18 surgeries in faraway hospitals, in hopes of saving his vision first, and then his eye. Though I was scared before the first surgery, I tried to be strong for William and Stacey. I could see Stacey was having a very hard time. God was dealing with him the same way He was dealing with me. William's surgeon, Dr. Michael Murphy, came in and explained the procedure. Then he got on his knees, held my hand and William's, and prayed for God to be the physician and guide his hand. I knew at that moment everything would be fine; God was in control.

"After more than 18 months of surgeries, William eventually lost sight and suffered the death of his eye. He now has to wear a prosthetic eye. Though it was a tragedy, we've had so many experiences where God has blessed us."

Karen counts it a blessing that she worked for nine years for Dr. Murphy, who mentored her in ophthalmology, work ethics, and Christian growth. She says he had inspirational faith: "He not only could talk the talk, but he also could and did walk the walk. I grew spiritually while I worked with him. Because of my experiences, I was able to help another mom whose son had a penetrating eye injury." What a blessing!

Karen also tells of people God put in their path who prayed and supported them—a pastor who didn't know them, and an unknown man in the cafeteria who prayed with Stacey during one of William's surgeries, and mysteriously appeared later. Karen says, "God knew what we needed and He provided. My faith grew as never before. My husband and I grew even closer. This experience actually strengthened our marriage, our family, and our walk with the Lord. I know God had a plan; He used this to draw me closer to Him and to grow me spiritually, shaping our lives tremendously for the Lord. I'm blessed to tell you that as a family we attend church and that our relationship with God first—and then with each other—is stronger."

And William? He's getting married, and never lets his blindness prevent a full life.

Joy When Life Is Upside-Down

Another champion of the Way, Renee Scheidt, popular speaker, and author, is filled with hope and joy in spite of a tragedy that happened to her in 1987. She says, "Without warning, in a mere few seconds, the life I had known as I followed God's leading was suddenly stripped from me. Never in my wildest imaginations would I have believed such devastation would be allowed to invade my world. What started as a dream-come-true concluded like a nightmare. Chuck, my minister-husband, ended his life with a gunshot wound to his head. For the previous eight weeks, he had been hospitalized as he struggled with a new diagnosis: bipolar disorder. Only one week after his release, his struggle ended. Mine was only beginning.

"At age 32, I found myself pushed into categories that sounded repulsive to me: widow, single-again, and hardest of all, single parent. Our precious babies, Nicole and Tara, were both under 3 years old when their daddy died.

"Staring in disbelief at the ashes of the past 12 years and struggling with emotions I didn't even know dwelt in my body, I somehow knew there was one major question I must answer before I could even begin to think about dealing with anything else. All other issues would be based on my response to this one question: What was I going to do with God?

"The fact that I was a Bible college and seminary graduate, and had been in ministry all my adult life, meant that I was grounded in the Scriptures. For years, I had proclaimed that God's Word was truth, and therefore, we should base our lives upon it. I had claimed the promise of eternal life by faith in Christ as a 17-year-old, and eagerly shared with others how they, too, could know they had a home in heaven. Without hesitation, I declared God's goodness and concern for His children.

"However, after Chuck died, I found that all I could see, feel, or understand stood in direct opposition to what I had previously affirmed. Is God still good when one's life is turned upside-down? Do God's promises remain true when it appears they simply can't be? A simple choice stood before me: all or nothing at all. Believe God—in spite of what I see, feel, and think—or walk away from Him. No middle ground. Walk by faith, or to hell with it all.

"Nineteen years later, I'm still here, proclaiming God's Word is true, and God is good. I've seen God rebuild the ruins I sat upon so many years ago. No, it hasn't been easy, but He's given me everything I've needed to keep on walking. The process has taken me places I never expected to go. To my surprise, I found that stumbling blocks can become stepping stones that are the pathway to heights I've never envisioned.

"And guess what? The good news is that God can do the same for you! The promise of Romans 8:28 is true—in spite of it all. Will you keep the faith during these tough times? It's a choice you'll never regret."

Read Romans 8:28. How has this principle been true in your life?

_____

_____

_____

_____

Read Matthew 11:28 and explain it in your own words.

_____

_____

_____

_____

Have you accepted God's will for you in troubled times?

_____

_____

_____

_____

How have you glorified Him even when things go wrong?

_____

_____

_____

_____

Do you see the characteristics from Study 3 in the three maturing Christian women in this study?

1. They accepted being in harness with Christ—even in troubled times.
2. They didn't resist the yoke, but were submissive.
3. Through Him, the burdens of life were easier.
4. They had hope for the future and joy in spite of tragedy.

Dietrich Bonhoeffer said the church in his day was selling a false doctrine of "cheap grace." As a mature Christian, you'll know how costly grace is—and *usually you'll know it's so much more than you can ever know.* Though you understand the danger, risk, and sadness, you show your faith in Christ in troubled times by your acts of obedience, love for others, and joyful heart through it all. You're *unrealistic,* according to the standard logic of the world, with a total trust, dependence, and unexplainably joyous victory in Jesus!

M & M: *Ministry and Missions Moment*

Martin Luther said, "Contrary to all that you choose or contrive or desire—that is the road you must take . . . the way of the cross. . . . You can't find it yourself. Jesus has to lead you as He would a blind man." You smile all the way. May the Lord make your life joyful as you see the path revealed along the way of the cross. As He leads this week, look for a ministry to someone in crisis.

Unit 2

———————•———————

DREAMING THROUGH THE TEARS

The Lord of your life is also the Lord of your dreams. Instead of looking down at the dirt beneath your feet, you dare look up and hope for the future. The deeper you delve into His Spirit, the higher you soar. In spite of a world full of trouble, as a Christian, you can find love, hope, and peace through submission to our Lord. In addition, He sends guidance through godly examples all around you, giving you hope for a bright future.

Through a Christian's look at the future, you can understand your mortality and come to terms with the transience of life. Recognizing that God and His Word are indestructible is the first step in relinquishing control over your life and submitting it to Him. Even when you're up against the dichotomies of life, experiencing the tensions between grief and joy, light and dark, good and evil, you find peace that passes all understanding as He cares for you.

. . . .

O Lord, you know I like to dream
Of future times. What will they be?
Will they be filled from day to day
With hope and faith and charity?
    Whatever place You bring me to,
    I trust you, Lord, to care for me.

                    —ee

. . . .

——— Study 6 ———

A Future in Him: A God of Hope

As I write this chapter, my Aunt Alice is dying in the hospital. Losing her husband at an early age, she's survived the single parenting of three boys, loss of income, death of other family members, upheavals at church, and loss of community in a changing neighborhood. Most tragic of all, she's had cancer for more than 40 years, yet her doctor has shaken his head in amazement many times, as her church members' intercessory prayer, God's intervention, and her faith have intersected in her healing. Though she has had unswerving hope—being in remission from ovarian cancer, uterine cancer, lung cancer, groin cancer, pancreatic cancer—she now is facing the last stages of this disease at age 79. I can honestly say that she and her sister (my mother) knew how to live and how to die. "Your word, O Lord, is eternal. It stands firm in the heavens. Your faithfulness continues though all generations" (Psalm 119:89–90).

Aunt Alice said to me recently, "Edna, you know it doesn't matter which way this comes out."

"Yes. I know."

"I have all hope and all peace."

"Yes."

"And it's worth it, just to know the Lord."

I couldn't respond. Tears of joy were streaming down my cheeks. When she dies, I won't be mourning. I'll be rejoicing because of her ecstatic joy in meeting her Savior face-to-face! I'm confident of the same joy in my husband, who died at age 48.

Hope in the Word

Christians who have faith at death's door and who have survived disasters tell of a deep sense of hope even in the midst of troubled days. Many of them have found hope in Scriptures. God's Word is a stabilizing force in times of chaos. In your hour of hurt, you can meditate on these principles about God's Word:

1. He's always near you. "You are near, O Lord, and all your commands are true" (Psalm 119:151).
2. When you hurt, He cares; He hurts *with you* and *for you.* "In all their distress he too was distressed" (Isaiah 63:9*a*).
3. He carries you through each crisis. "In his love and mercy he redeemed them; he lifted them up and carried them" (Isaiah 63:9*b*).
4. God sends His Spirit to give you rest from life's journey—even in the midst of chaos. "They were given rest by the Spirit of the Lord" (Isaiah 63:14).

Read the following Scriptures and explain in your own words what each says about God's Word giving you hope.
Isaiah 40:6-8

_____

_____

Hebrews 7:16

_____

_____

Hebrews 13:8

_____

_____

Indestructible Scripture

When talking with His enemies, Jesus said, "The Scripture cannot be broken" (John 10:35). The Greek word for _broken_ means "being separated." A horrible fact about tragedy and chaos is that they isolate you from others. In the interest of privacy, and fearing shame, you often can't share your hurt with even your best friend. Nothing seems permanent and steady. However, God steadies and strengthens you—and may be doing that right now—as you find comfort in Scripture. Hope comes through the assurance that Scripture is indestructible. You can depend on it!

Scripture cannot separate; instead it rejoins you with God. As Jesus did, you find answers to those who persecute you and peace in any situation that troubles you. You even find hope and happiness in God's fellowship _when you've lost the fellowship of everyone else who's important in your life!_

Scripture Leads Us to the Indestructible Christ

A major strength found in your Bible is that all of it leads us to Christ. First-century Christians pointed to the Old Testament verses as a foreshadowing of Christ, who fulfilled the law and truth in the Old Testament. For centuries the Israelites had tried to please God by appeasing Him. Their priestly tribe, the Levites, served for centuries as tabernacle mediators with God. Then when Christ came, He became the perfect mediator for the Hebrews (Hebrews 8:6). Since He died for all sin, He humbled Himself to perform the ultimate sacrifice as He became the Holy Lamb. "Christ also did not take upon himself the glory of becoming a high priest, but God said to him, 'You are my Son'. . . . And he says in another place, 'You are a priest forever'" (Hebrews 5:5-6). He has "become a priest not on the basis of a regulation as to his ancestry but on the basis of the power of an indestructible life" (Hebrews 7:16). Because of His resurrection, Jesus proved Himself indestructible, and He promises all Christians are indestructible too: "I give them eternal life, and they shall never perish; no one can snatch them out of my hand" (John 10:28). One major calming force in my life during the times I've walked through troubled waters has been Scripture.

Write your favorite verses that give you hope in times of trouble.

_____

_____

If appropriate, share them with a friend, study partner, or someone going through troubled times.

Here are my favorite verses for troubled times:

- ❧ "And we know that in all things God works for the good of those who love him, who have been called according to his purpose" (Romans 8:28).
- ❧ "Long ago I learned from your statutes that you established them to last forever" (Psalm 119:152).
- ❧ "What then, shall we say in response to this? If God is for us, who can be against us?" (Romans 8:31).
- ❧ "Who shall separate us from the love of Christ? Shall trouble or hardship or persecution or famine or nakedness or danger or sword? . . . No, in all these things we're more than conquerors through him who loves us" (Romans 8:35, 37).
- ❧ "And we rejoice in the hope of the glory of God. Not only so, but we also rejoice in our sufferings, because we know that

suffering produces perseverance; perseverance, character; and character, hope" (Romans 5:2b-4).

Because Scripture, dependable and unbreakable, stands firmly on the promises of Jesus the indestructible, we have cause for solid hope. Because "Jesus Christ is the same yesterday and today and forever" (Hebrews 13:8), we trust Him to be actively, solidly, and permanently working in our lives for good—regardless of dire circumstances we see.

Futurecasting in Christ's Hope

One exciting activity invented in the twentieth century is *future-casting*. I've done futurecasting in several secular as well as religious settings. Usually a group gathers to futurecast, but one person can do it. You may hear famous secular personalities talk about "reinventing" themselves. Futurecasting is a kind of prediction of future trends based not on what is logically probable, but what is personally preferable. On the Internet (especially on blogs) you'll find futurecasting attempts on every subject, from what the United Nations can do in Afghanistan to anticipation of combining all electronic/wireless equipment to provide music and communication for future generations (and profits for investors, of course).

As Christians futurecast, they pray and then pool their spiritual sensings about what God is going to do. They depend on *God to reinvent them*, not relying on their own power to reinvent themselves. Differing from forecasting, which is a thinking (cognitive) anticipation of the future using probabilities based on current conditions, Christian futurecasting is an intuitive, prayerful expectation of the future, using your own volition combined with God's will. Futurecasting is not forecasting with a few facts embellished.

As a Christian, you can use futurecasting to predict trends, not in the secular world but in your own heart. You can build a conceptual model of your life as God nudges you forward, not trusting your plans, but aligning your will with His. It is vitally important that you submit your will to God's overseeing will for your life as you record your ideas for this futuristic model.

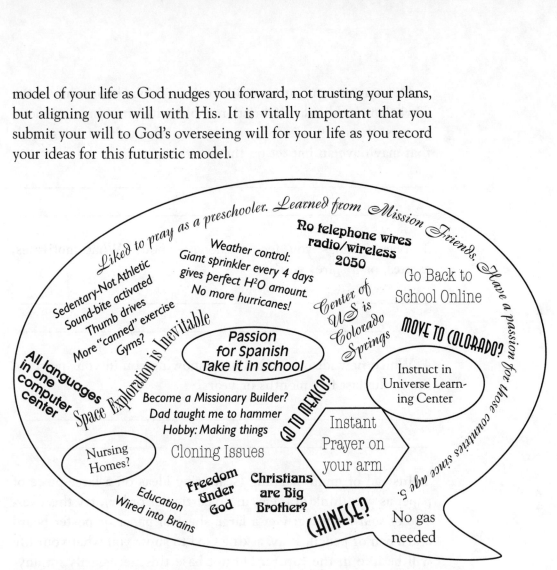

Steps to Futurecasting

1. Pray, asking God to bring to your mind things you need to know for future hope. Record thoughts, ideas, or strong feelings He impresses on your mind.

_____

_____

2. Do you see innovative and futuristic things happening in the Christian world today (Christian books with stunning new ideas, pastors' thoughts, missions trends, breakthroughs of the gospel) that may have an impact on the future?

_____

_____

3. Name things you feel passionate about. What motivates, excites, or inspires you?

_____

_____

4. Which new ideas has God been showing you in your personal life in the last few months or years?

_____

_____

5. Instead of mind-mapping (scattering ideas on a large piece of paper as you think of them, in no particular order), try this exercise of *soul-mapping*: Get a large sheet of paper or poster board and a pen or pencil. Pray, asking God to show you what your life will be like in the future. Do not base this necessarily on anything you do in everyday life presently (see previous page). Ask God to show you how the passion He's given you may materialize in the future. Write all His "nudges" or ideas: upside down, sideways, jotted in margins, and so on, as they come to mind.

_____

_____

_____

6. Prayerfully add from numbers 1 through 4 any ideas you feel you need on your soul-mapping "nudges." Then see if any new thoughts you now have fit any spot on the soul-map.

7. Pray. Set aside what you've written on the large sheet (or poster board) for at least 24 hours. Then ask God to help you delete, add, and prioritize His nudges.

8. Using your chosen priorities, design a futurecast for 30 years from this date, setting a minimum of tentative goals on ministry and service to God. Use these areas to delineate a preferred probability for the future.

Spiritual Futurecast Matrix:
What would you like to see in 30 years in the following areas?

Prayer	Worship
Daily Praise Time with God	Personal Purity
Family Life	Other Relationships
Forgiveness	Mercy
Love	Joy
Realistic Ministry	Outrageously Optimistic Ministry
Work	Giving
Learning Opportunities	Hobbies
Sacrificial Service to Others	Sacrificial Service to God
Other:	Other:

9. Take your time, and write a one-paragraph summary of your preferred spiritual future as a Christian 30 years from now.

_____

_____

_____

_____

_____

_____

_____

_____

_____

_____

_____

_____

_____

10. Pray for His guidance and plans for your future. Cast your hope and faith in the future, aligning your will to God's perfect will. Now, follow His plan.

What a joy to futurecast about Aunt Alice! She radiates hope already. As we look into the future, we can see hope and light. "The grass withers and the flowers fall, but the word of our God stands forever" (Isaiah 40:8).

M & M: *Ministry and Missions Moment*

Whether you futurecast alone or with a group of study friends, you can reach a preferred prediction of your spiritual life with God. Find a group and futurecast this week. Approaching the future with hope, increase the depth of your relationship with Him, the author of all hope.

——— Study 7 ———

Trust in Others: God-Given Guidance

A little girl said to her mother, "I know I can pray to God, who's with me in my dark room, but can you stay for a while? I need to see God with skin on." You, too, need godly friends to give you guidance. Especially in troubled times, they're a voice of reason and comfort.

As you search for guidance from godly Christians, you will find many variables.

Changing Trends

"In today's world, it's hard to hope in others," said Sheryl, "because even among Christians, you seldom find dependability." Statistics on people under 55 show Christians break their own code of ethics. Their lives don't follow God's law consistently. Also, because women are so busy, they have little time to mentor or be mentored. In addition, we live in such a transient society that women have no mothers or aunts nearby who can guide them. Women today—as self-assured as they seem—desperately need God-given guidance from godly women. Christian moral codes may have changed in some areas, but you may be just what women like Sheryl are looking for: a dependable, maturing woman.

Generational Differences

For the first time in history, as many as five generations of women can be found living in the same family. Tricia Scribner, author of *Unity in Diversity* and co-author of *Woman to Woman: Preparing Yourself to Mentor*, says, "As a nurse I used to see 50-year-old daughters bringing their 70-year-old mothers to the doctor. Today we often see 70-year-old daughters bringing their 90-year-old mothers. Because we live longer, we have many more mentoring opportunities."

What kind of trends do you see in your neighborhood? Write several here.

_____

_____

Discuss these changing times with a study friend or your pastor.

Are you a member of the sandwich generation, caring for parents and children at the same time? _____

How do you cope with the tough times? Write words of advice here.

_____

_____

_____

_____

Mentoring Needs

A young woman today needs help. Many expect her to be to be a multi-talented supermom. She faces the impossible job of being a working mother (sometimes single mom) with the cleanups, carpools, and homework with her children. Housekeeping help is prohibitively expensive. Though her husband may pitch in, helping with childcare and housecleaning, most women take major responsibility for children and meals. Though she may desire an ethical Christian life, she may find pornography coming inside her home through television shows and computer programming. In addition, she lives in a culture where law enforcement struggles to prosecute child molesters who use the Internet to invite her children to a rendezvous, where they will be mistreated or killed. Compared to the way I reared my children as a stay-at-home mom in the safe, small town where I'd grown up, today's woman is often terrified.

If she chooses not to work outside the home, she may face financial crises. If she takes on home schooling, she adds mental and physical strains. Her isolation causes a yearning for entertainment, spiritual encouragement, fellowship with other adults, and help with the psychological and spiritual nurturing of her children. Because of today's transience, she often doesn't have family to assist her. While coed couples' classes at church build marriage strength, they may make it less likely that a woman will have a place to talk with other women in a safe, Christian environment.

Although crises may strengthen some marriages as a couple unites to meet the challenge, it is more likely the stress and exhaustion causes disillusionment and marital burnout. Without counseling and prayer, the marriage may face failure.

Mentoring Challenges

You'd probably agree that the overworked woman needs a mentor to help her, but because of the two major generation *gaps* (Silent Generation years, 1940–1945; and Baby Buster years, 1964–1979) many women are isolated between generations. One factor that impedes helpful mentoring is the almost-universal negative attitude about pride among older Christians. When I was a child, during the World War II/Korean War eras, children grew up hearing "You're getting too big for your britches," or "You need taking down a peg or two." As a result, my generation had little self-esteem. Church leaders taught us pride was the worst trait in a Christian woman.

When a younger woman experiencing stress asks an older woman to mentor her, the older is apt to decline, not because she's too busy, but because she thinks she has nothing to offer or she thinks mentoring is too prideful. National surveys and informal anecdotes confirm she may be afraid to give comfort during troubled times because of feelings of inadequacy.

If you've never been a mentor, what is holding you back? Explain.

_____

_____

_____

_____

_____

_____

Mentoring Opportunities

Though the outlook seems bleak for postmodern women, you can find help and give help to others. First, look around you. Which women in your church, neighborhood, or work place seem overwhelmed? What are they seeking? Look back at Study 6 and see if the passion in your futurecast interfaces with the need for mentoring in your area. Whether or not you *need* a mentor, every woman needs to *be* mentoring. For example, a 20-something woman should be mentoring a preteen or teen; a 60-something should be mentoring a 40-something, an 80-something should be mentoring a 60-something, and so on. Each stage of your life presents an opportunity to mentor someone in crisis, depression, or a pre-crisis stage.

Pre-crisis Mentoring

You may offer to mentor someone in the pre-crisis stage, to prevent later burnout and depression. Pray as you look around you, asking God to lead you to (1) a mentor and (2) a *merea* (Hebrew; pronounced "Mah-RAY-ah," meaning dear young friend; probably used by Ruth and her mother-in-law, Naomi, in the Old Testament). You need relationships with all ages of women.

Informal mentoring takes place daily. In fact, we can't totally organize this *God thing,* superimposing our rules. However, there are some formal mentoring opportunities you can find. Christian Women's Job Corps (CWJC) offers a well-organized Christian environment for lifting women up to self-sufficiency with hope for the future for themselves and their children. (For more information, visit the Web site at www.wmu.com/VolunteerConnection/cwjc; email CWJC@wmu.org; or call (205) 991-8100.)

Dog and Flea Volunteer Mentoring

You can also mentor others in a volunteer service job, such as disaster relief. Donna Swartz of Magee, Mississippi, has mentored Susie Rawls for years, and they've gone on many trips. During the Hurricane Katrina disaster, Donna was made the first woman White Hat, a disaster relief site coordinator. Donna and Susie once called me and said, "Hello, this is your dog and flea from Mississippi! We just returned from Minnesota!" They'd helped with flood relief, one of many jobs they tackled successfully. They explained: a good mentor takes others with her like a dog takes fleas wherever it goes.

You can take a younger woman along with you whether you're volunteering with disaster relief, delivering Meals on Wheels, building a Habitat for Humanity house, or sorting clothes at the Salvation Army. Whatever you volunteer to do, invite someone to go with you. A young woman once told me she sat at home watching other women come and go with volunteer work at a church across the street from her house. She needed to get out of the house, but was too shy to go by herself or ask someone else to take her along. She was thrilled when some women asked her to join them. Houses are full of women yearning for companionship and encouragement. You can bless them through God-given guidance. In spite of statistics that show Christians aren't dependable because they break their own code of ethics, you can become trustworthy and others will trust you. Then you can change the world, guiding one woman at a time.

Mentoring Roles

You can mentor in one or more of these five roles:

1. **Servant:** You can minister to another woman by providing a ride to church, inviting her to your home for coffee, connecting her to a community service (clothes or food bank), giving her a phone number, or helping set up tables for her club meeting.

2. **Encourager:** Minister to a woman by verbally affirming her and cheering her on. Send her a note of encouragement or give her an award for achievement.

3. **Teacher:** Share your knowledge of Christ in an informal way as you become friends. Give her Scripture notes/cards to memorize. Use a two-by-two Bible study (see Study 18) to teach her painlessly the biblical principles by which she can live her life. Help with errors in her thinking and clarify God's words, as you've been taught.

4. **Counselor:** Everyone needs a friend to listen. Especially in the

tough times of life, you can give advice with her interest at heart. She may need your nurturing, or she may need professional counseling to which you can refer her. Most likely, she just needs a friend.

5. **Guide:** You've been where a younger woman has not gone. You can model the Christian walk and help her follow the path. You can model failure as well as success. She needs to know what happens when a Christian like you fails, dusts yourself off, gets up, and tries again. If you think you've failed too many times and you're not qualified to mentor, think again. Your failure qualifies you as one who can guide someone else who's recently failed. You've been there. (For more about Christian guidance, see Study 26).

In which of the mentoring roles above would you feel comfortable?

_____

_____

In which would you feel uncomfortable?

_____

_____

Is God calling you into a mentoring role? Pray that you'll be able to discern His will.

M & M: Ministry and Missions Moment

Trust in others and you're a merea. Let them trust in you and you're a mentor. Go along with someone else like a flea on a dog, and you're a merea. Take someone else along like a dog with fleas and you're a mentor. God-given guidance is a two-way street. How about it? Will you say yes as He leads you to do both this week?

Study 8

Encompassing the World: The Love of God

When asked why she served in Asia, a missionary responded: "I grew up like many in America—loved listening to music for hours; shopping for shoes, makeup, and the latest fashions. I guess you'd say I was totally self-centered. I said I'd die if I didn't have the right brand of jeans or sneakers, and I hung out all day with friends without thinking of anything but myself. Then one summer my best friend died in a car accident. At the funeral I realized something was wrong with my life. For days afterward, I cried and refused to go out of my room. One Sunday, my mom talked me into going to church with her. I wept throughout the service, and afterward talked a moment with the pastor in his office. He gave me a book by Peter Marshall called *Mr. Jones, Meet the Master*. In it I found the most amazing story about an ordinary man, whom God tapped on the shoulder. The man, Mr. Jones, made a 180-degree turn, following God. He walked in that opposite direction from that day forward. I realized I needed to do what Mr. Jones did. I read Scriptures the pastor had given me and asked Jesus Christ into my heart. I promised Him I would walk in His direction from that moment on."

Love that Lingers

Then the missionary described her change of direction: "What happened next was incredible. I felt overflowing happiness. The dark depression I'd had for weeks left instantly. The presence of Christ lingered. When I saw my old friends the next day, they seemed shallow. What they talked about seemed like filthy gossip. Somehow my heart had changed. I loved other people, and it hurt me to hear my friends saying unkind things. When anyone called God's name in vain, I felt wounded and deeply sad. My whole perspective on God and people had been transformed.

"As months passed, I took a night job, went to seminary, and learned everything I could about God: His Word—in Hebrew and Greek—the history of His work through the ages, and everything He was doing in today's world. While I studied, my heart was drawn to a people group in Asia. I was compelled to love them. I came here because I could do nothing else. God pulled my heart in this direction, and I'm just following Him. That happened years ago, and God's presence still lingers and fills my heart with love."

A Natural Walk in Love

Once God takes sovereignty over a heart, it responds in love. Some say God's love is indiscriminate: He loves everything He created. *Everything*. Just as God loves, His followers love. Because He indwells them, His love flows through them to all people. They love indiscriminately. A godly woman in my neighborhood, "Grams," illustrated this principle well. She had wealthy friends whom she loved; everyone expected those relationships to work, and they did. However, she also had several relationships that my other neighbors considered strange. She befriended a Hispanic man who did yard work in her next-door neighbor's yard. I often saw her take him a glass of lemonade and ask about his children. Occasionally she sent a gift to his wife. Grams established a friendship with an elderly single man of a different race who'd recently had a leg removed. Some said their relationship was a scandal since she was a widow. She took an ample lunch to his home every day, with enough leftovers for dinner. She vowed she'd take food to him until he died, regardless of what others said, and she did.

She reached out to the meanest little child in the neighborhood, who threw rocks at humans and animals alike. He loved to listen to stories about her childhood. She also loved the aloof calico cat, who made little cat footprints all over our cars. Tiger, our dog who barked at everyone, strangely didn't bark at Grams, who petted animals and talked in a gentle voice as they listened. Grams was like Albert Schweitzer, who wouldn't step on an ant because it was one of God's creatures. She had a respect for every flower, animal, and human being. *She walked in love.* Such love is a natural walk for maturing Christians.

When you allow God to fill your heart, you'll be so joyful that troubles and sin cannot engulf you. Love fills all the nooks and crannies, leaving no room there for whining about your troubles. When you reach out to love others, you forget about your own issues and begin the natural walk of love that leads to service.

Do you know someone like Grams? Describe her (or him).

_____

_____

How do you walk the natural walk of love in your neighborhood? Explain.

_____

_____

_____

Love that Breaks Barriers

Not only do hearts of love reach out to neighborhoods, but also they reach out to the world. Most Christians find new horizons for love as they go on mission trips, teach internationals to speak English, or move to a new culture in another place. They're willing to go to a Third World country to serve God, as He leads. Jesus says, "You will receive power when the Holy Spirit comes on you; and you will be my witnesses in Jerusalem, and in all Judea and Samaria, and to the ends of the earth" (Acts 1:8).

When does Jesus say you'll receive power?

_____

Once you're empowered with the love of God flowing through your inner heart, what will you do?

_____

_____

In which area(s) does your service to God move?

_____

_____

How do these areas compare to your home area?

_____

_____

Jesus also said, "All authority in heaven and on earth has been given to me. Therefore go and make disciples of all nations, baptizing them in the name of the Father and of the Son and of the Holy

Spirit, and teaching them to obey everything I have commanded you. And surely I am with you always, to the very end of the age" (Matthew 28:18–20).

What authority compels you to go and make disciples of all nations?

_____

_____

_____

According to these verses, name the steps Jesus lists for you to take as you walk the natural walk of love and break barriers of time and space:

1. Therefore, _____

2. And make disciples of _____

3. Baptizing them in the _____

    a) _____

    b) _____

    c) _____

4. And teaching them to _____

_____ .

How long will God be with you, living in your heart?

_____

_____

_____

_____

Love that Encompasses the World

Kay Wilson, in Clinton, Mississippi, a teaching nurse who has mentored many younger women in missions and ministry, has traveled all over the world, going to India and other places to work in hospitals, especially ministering to the poor and needy with medical concerns. She once told me, "If God calls me, I don't worry about the risk in a dangerous area. I don't worry about receiving the funds for the long journey overseas. I don't worry about rearranging my schedule to take the time off to go. If God calls me, He takes care of all that. I just go and nurse people who are sick or teach nursing in the hospitals to which He calls me." Kay is a good example of a woman who has encompassed the world with the love of God. She shares Him wherever she goes.

M & M: Ministry and Missions Moment

Pray around the world this week, remembering those who are sick and hurting as you read headlines or watch worldwide news programs. Decide on one place where you can minister to someone who needs God's love; then follow His words, "Therefore, go."

— Study 9 —

It Passes Understanding: The Peace of God

A poor family in North Vietnam celebrated the premature birth of a girl they named Quyna. Because of her small size, family and friends nicknamed her "Little One." When she was a teen, North Vietnam officers arrested Quyna, accusing her of helping the enemy. Innocent but afraid for her life, she escaped on the last ship leaving for South Vietnam, where American missionary Betty Merrell befriended her. She also met an American GI, Dave Carpenter; they fell in love, and Betty's husband, Ron, married the young couple. As South Vietnam fell and Quyna and Dave left Vietnam for America, he promised that one day they'd be able to go back and find her mother and two sisters. Quyna had great faith and felt peaceful, knowing she was in God's hands.

Dave and Quyna settled in America as active members of a Christian church. Eventually, they saved enough money to return to North Vietnam. They took with them, the Jesus film, flyers to help them locate their family, and witnessing tracts for sharing with Vietnamese people. Meanwhile their friends in America prayed that Quyna would find her long-lost family. Initially, their family searches seemed to lead nowhere. Then friends invited them to come to their vacation house for a holiday. Dave and Quyna experienced extraordinary peace within.

When the couple arrived at the vacation house, the phone rang: Quyna's nephew quickly answered all their questions, calling her "Little One." Sadly, he told Quyna her mother had died, along with one of her sisters, but soon she was united with the other sister, her son—the nephew who had called—and other extended family. Though she'd never been able to see her mother again, Quyna had great joy and peace that they could share Jesus with other Vietnamese.

Returning to the US, Dave and Quyna continued to save money for yearly trips. On one visit, they took equipment for irrigation so villages could grow crops for food. They also took school supplies. Each year they found more Christians, rejoicing that the Christian soldiers who had come earlier in the century had made an impact on the Vietnamese.

Peace within the Heartbreak of War

Though war and other chaos always cause heartbreak, a strange phenomenon takes place in the broken heart of a Christian: she's at peace in the midst of the worst imaginable situation. Just as Bonhoeffer (Study 2) and others shared their faith during wartime and received the reward of heart-peace with Jesus, Dave and Quyna experienced inexplicable peace and deep joy as they walked in the Spirit, not in the flesh. Also, though she was absent from her Christian family and friends from time to time, Quyna could say as Paul did, "Though I am absent from you in body, I am present with you in spirit and delight to see how . . . firm your faith in Christ is" (Colossians 2:5).

These words from Paul explain a *dichotomy that illustrates a tension in the Christian life:* Absent from the body, but present with you in spirit.

Death: Sacrifice on Earth—
Life: Reward in Heaven

Christianity is filled with many dichotomies: Satan/God; evil/good;

death/life; sacrifice/reward. For those Jesus mentioned who would suffer persecution for their faith, He promises "in the age to come, eternal life" (Mark 10:30). When you sacrifice your own personality, reputation, or lifeblood for the cause of Christ, you will find Christ's comfort and peace. For every sacrifice you make, He promises you'll be rewarded with eternal life in heaven.

Rewards come in many forms: recognition, justice, peace, ethical satisfaction, affirmation, self-confidence . . . the list is endless. However, the most important reward is having a relationship with Almighty God. Think of it: you can have a personal relationship with the Creator, who sends His Spirit as your advocate-comforter! *Jesus experienced the reward of joy—of knowing that you'd experience eternal life through His sacrifice. You can experience the reward of joy, too, with a deeper personal relationship with your Lord.* The second half of John 15:11 reads "And that your joy may be complete." As you learned in Study 4, His joy in you is reciprocal, as He becomes alive in you and makes you alive.

Duality of Spirit

In Romans 8, Paul explains a duality of spirits in each person: "Those who live according to the sinful nature [flesh, KJV] have their minds set on what that nature desires; but those who live in accordance with the Spirit have their minds set on what the Spirit desires. The mind of sinful man is death, but the mind controlled by the Spirit is life and peace" (Romans 8:5-6).

Since all humans were born into a sinful world because of the Fall, we feel comfortable in sin. It is beautiful and feels good.

Do you agree that sin is beautiful? Give examples.

_____

_____

Do you agree that sin feels good? Give examples.

_____

_____

_____

_____

Reread Romans 8:5-6. List what you believe are carnal nature desires. _____

_____

List what you believe the Spirit desires.

_____

_____

Scriptures give us information about the dichotomy of evil or good, flesh or spirit. Instead of being clothed in sin, we're clothed in Christ (Galatians 3:27). Instead of possessing impurity leading to wickedness, you possess "righteousness leading to holiness" (Romans 6:19).

Read Romans 8:2. Instead of following "the law of sin and death," you follow:

_____

_____

Instead of having your mind on sinful nature's desire (Romans 8:5), you have your mind set on:

_____

_____

Instead of being dead in your body (Romans 8:10), you are:

_____

_____

Instead of having a spirit of slavery (Romans 8:15–16), you have:

_____

_____

Instead of just shared suffering (Romans 8:17), you have:

_____

_____

Instead of concentrating on your present suffering (Romans 8:18), you concentrate on:

_____

_____

Instead of being frustrated by Satan (Romans 8:20–21), you are liberated, brought into:

_____

_____

Other Scriptures also describe the dichotomy. As you witness, you'll sow spiritual seeds to reap a material harvest (1 Corinthians 9:11). Instead of using deadly weapons, you'll receive spiritual weapons for spiritual warfare (2 Corinthians 10:3–5). Instead of fruits of the flesh, horribly described in Galatians 5:19-21, you'll receive fruits of the Spirit: love, joy, peace, patience, kindness, goodness, faithfulness, gentleness and self-control (Galatians 5:22–23). What a list of blessings!

Your life, as long as you live in this world, will have these two-sided tensions pulling you one way or the other: Walking in darkness or walking in light; wise in the eyes of the world or foolish for God; weak in the body or strong in the Spirit. . . in short, living for Satan or for God.

Evil or Good, Flesh or Spirit

Our sinful nature is attracted to evil, rather than good. Paul says, "So I find this law at work: When I want to do good, evil is right there with me" (Romans 7:21).

How do you feel when you get revenge on someone who has continued to irritate you? Does it feel good? How do you feel when you win an argument? Does it satisfy you? How does a smoker feel when she sees cigarettes (or an obese person when she sees desserts)? Do they look beautiful? An adulterer sees a lover as more beautiful than a godly spouse. Satan makes sin alluring and enticing.

The Winning Factor: In-Living

Since it's undeniable that humans find sin enticing, we have no hope except for one factor—in-living—that is, the indwelling of the Living God inside us. In Romans 8 above, Paul uses the Greek word, *pneuma*, or Spirit. He identifies the location of this Spirit in Romans 7:22: "For in my inner being I delight in God's law; but I see another law at work in the members of my body, waging war against the law of my mind and making me a prisoner of the law of sin at work within my members." Here's Paul's delight: God's law *in his inner being*. Like Paul, dear Christian woman, in your deepest spirit, the Spirit of God dwells. There He stores the Word, to keep you on track in your walk in the Spirit, in spite of nagging tendencies to sin, which we've inherited from Adam and Eve.

The Secret of Christian Living

First Corinthians 3:16 reads, "You . . . are God's temple . . . God's Spirit lives in you." Because you aren't able to see the world as God sees it, you can understand this mystery only through *spiritual discernment*. Jesus said, "The world cannot accept him [the Spirit] because it neither sees him or knows him. But you know him, for he lives with you and will be *in you*. . . . On that day [when Jesus is in heaven, and the Holy Spirit comes to live in your heart], you will realize that I am *in my Father*, and you are *in me* and I am *in you*" (John 14:17–20). Jesus says, "Remain in me" (John 15:4).

Define and describe "in-living" in your own words.

_____

_____

_____

_____

Looking Up, Looking Out

In-living is not an earthly condition. "Since, then, you have been raised with Christ. . . set your minds on things above, not on earthly things" (Colossians 3:1–2). To keep heavenward, you will relinquish flesh and accept Spirit every day. Paul says, "Put off your old self, which is being corrupted by its deceitful desires; to be made new [literally, *exchanged*] in the attitude of your minds; and . . . put on the new self, created to be like God in true righteousness" (Ephesians 4:22).

Paul wanted his converts to look up, but also look out, cooperating with the people of God. He says to Christians in Corinth, "Brothers, I could not address you as spiritual but as worldly—mere infants in Christ. . . . For since there is jealousy and quarreling among you, are you not worldly?" (1 Corinthians 3:1, 3). God tells us, "Make every effort to keep the unity of the Spirit through the bond of peace" (Ephesians 4:3). The peace we give each other bonds us in unity, as unity with Christ gives peace with others and within ourselves.

The Proportions of Peace

Jesus said, "The kingdom of God is in you" (Luke 1:21). *Your peace is in direct proportion to the amount of in-living you've given to the Spirit in your life.* As Paul says above, "I pray that out of his glorious riches he may strengthen you with power through his Spirit *in your inner being*" (Ephesians 3:16). Once you've given place in your inner being for the in-living, you can say, "It is well with my soul."

M & M: *Ministry and Missions Moment*

Set aside time this week to pray for world peace and peace in our nation. Then pray for inner peace for people you know who are troubled. Share "The Proportions of Peace" above with someone this week.

—— Study 10 ——

In the Palm of His Hand: Submission to God

For years, I moved from place to place with an ornate studio piano, a large china cabinet, two beds—with accompanying dressers and chests of drawers—and assorted bicycles and outdoor tools. I justified that baggage by saying, "Surely, God, you don't want me to give away good things my children may be able to use." I saved the piano thinking Patsy would take it when she married. Then she married a man with a piano. I then saved it for my son, Jack, thinking he'd take it when he married. He married a woman who also owned a piano! Finally, I sold the piano. The day I sold it was an epiphany for me: I realized that piano had hung around my neck like an albatross! Without it, I was free. Today I own only one piece of furniture: a white wingback chair that sits near a bed I don't own in a bedroom in my daughter's home. I live there part of the time, in my son's home in Alabama, or on the road, traveling to women's conferences or mission trips. I have nothing hanging around my neck except the love of Christ, which comforts me.

What's hanging around your neck today, weighing you down? What hampers your serving Christ with every fiber of your being? Are you too old? Too young? Too encumbered? Too busy? Whatever you're using as an excuse not to serve God, it's no excuse. Serve Him at whatever He asks; live it with all your heart, witness to the goodness of Jesus whatever the circumstance.

Clinging to the "What Ifs" of Life

Every situation has some sadness and some joy. Yet many Christians remain in the infantile stages of spiritual growth because they cling to the "what ifs" of life. Many singles cling to the sad "What if I had married?" syndrome. Married women cling to the "What if I had married my first boyfriend?" syndrome. I meet many widows clinging to unbelievably false hopes that their dead husbands could come back to life! They waste valuable time—when they could be witnessing about God's goodness—as they mourn for dozens of years rather than accepting God's gift of widowhood: freedom from having to cook grits or oatmeal for a family at 6:00 A.M., freedom to manage your money, visit grandchildren, serve as a missionary overseas, or go on new adventures. Celebrating the little things makes troubled waters calm. God says, "If anyone acknowledges that Jesus is the Son of God, God lives in him and he in God" (1 John 4:15). Forgetting the "what ifs" and yielding to His will are essential for in-living experience.

Name a few "what ifs" you've used in the past.

_____

_____

Follow Jesus

So you want the peace that passes all understanding, as we discussed in Study 9? There's a way to obtain that, if you're willing to follow the right path. The path begins with two words: *follow Jesus*.

What did Jesus do in His lifetime?
1. He was born humble.
2. He dedicated Himself to be about His Father's business.
3. He came to earth to die.
4. He suffered.
5. He was willing to give everything for others.

How much of *everything* would you be willing to give? For years I struggled with the word *everything*. I was willing to move from my hometown after my husband died and my children were in college to serve God in a church-related vocation. I'd promised to follow Him wherever He led me, and He miraculously showed me where He wanted me to go. I later realized I was able to give Him more than I thought I could give. As years pass, you learn more about *everything* you can give.

The Gift of Little Things

Picture a woman bent over, carrying a heavy sack over her shoulder. Her sweater pockets are bulging with beautiful rocks that heavily weigh her down. On her head she balances a giant pot full of liquid, which she steadies with one hand, creating a weird balance as she bobbles along. In her other hand, she carries a walking stick to lean on as she struggles uphill. She never lays her burdens down, for when she tries to, they come alive, surround her, and whine until she picks them back up again. When she falls, she slowly, sadly gathers her burdens, rights herself—but never quite straight—and wobbles uphill.

Most of us are like this woman. The cares of the world burden us, to the point of falling. We dabble in sin until our hearts are heavy. We're disappointed and disillusioned with our families or our society—or even the clergy who lead us spiritually.

We receive over-stimulation from too many sounds and too many visuals; too much immorality—the bombardment of sin. We eat too much and drink too much, carry too much information and endure outrageous propaganda, with an overload of media images startling us every day. We continue to live in a blurred world, and we pile on our backs all sorts of kitchen gadgets like bread makers and food slicers and blenders and electric knives, along with super-portable hybrid phones and beepers, iPods and flash drives; and with each widget, we become more a part of the world. We drive vehicles with the latest features, and each family member has to have one, with an extra in the yard. A house is not a home without more add-ons each year or two: a dormer window here, an awning there.

The bent-over woman never made it up the hill. About halfway up, she saw a violet blooming at her feet. She leaned down to look at it, and the pot fell off her head. Ignoring the valuable liquid that spilled out all over the parched ground, she touched the velvet petals of the tiny violet. She stood in the sun, almost paralyzed by the violet, whose sweet smell wafted over the path. She took off her sweater and laid it down, forgetting the valuable stones in the pockets. She smelled the violet. Ah! It was a thing of beauty to see and to smell. Time passed, and she laid down her heavy sack holding precious possessions. Without the sack, she didn't need the walking stick! What freedom! She tried a hop, then a skip, then a dance! She twirled in the sunlight until it became moonlight. She wasn't tired anymore. She stood erect, without any fetters! She followed a light in the distance until it led her to perfect peace.

Do you know this woman? At times you may dream that you're this woman. You may recognize that possessions hold power over you. Only when you're free of heavy possessions can you walk upright.

Take Nothing for the Journey

When Jesus prepared His disciples to relinquish family and home to go as evangelistic missionaries in a hostile world, He said, "Take nothing for the journey" (Luke 9:3). Imagine in a land without public restaurants or hotels as we have today, Jesus saying, "take no purse, no bag, no bread, no money, no extra tunic." Today we might say, "take no BlackBerry, no iPod, no bling bling, no fancy shoes, no cell phone, no hair dryer, no credit cards, no cooler with sodas."

How easy would it be for you to go on a mission trip without the things listed above?

_____

_____

What would you require for travel?

_____

_____

You're Not in Charge

After having brain surgery in Eastern Europe, missionary Vesta Sauter sent an email: "These past two years have taught me so much, and among my many lessons has been to learn that I'm not in control; God, and God alone, is sovereign, and it's Him and Him alone who's in control. 'Trust in the Lord with all your heart and lean not on your own understanding; in all your ways acknowledge him, and he will make your paths straight'" (Proverbs 3:5–6 NKJV). Vesta is a person I admire for her servant attitude. She's set an example for women who've submitted to God's will and place themselves in the palm of His hand. I'm sure it's been hard for Vesta to relinquish control of her life. All of us find it hard to give up self, possessions, health, or family. We like to be in charge. However, if we're to be the godly women God's wants us to be, we praise Him, love Him, and submit to His will for our lives—through good and bad. He requires nothing less. John said, "Those who obey his commands live in him, and he in them" (1 John 3:24).

Linka Moore, a wonderful, godly teacher of our Sunday School class, said good-bye to her son, his wife, and children as they went on their way to Alaska to be missionaries. We discussed in our class how hard it must be not to be able to see her grandchildren, but Linka said in strong words of faith, "What could be a better place for them than in the palm of God's hand?" Hundreds of missionaries have left America for dangerous, faraway places. Yet parents as well as their adult children smile, submitting to the will of God, trusting themselves and their family members to the Lord.

Which of the following would you be able to submit to God's will?

Career	**Health**	**Parents**
Children	**Husband**	**Home**
Furniture	**Death in the family**	

The song, "This World Is Not My Home" points to heaven as the ultimate end to the path on which God leads you, since you're a citizen of heaven. Though you're not of the world, you live in the world, which sometimes calls you away from the path on which you might follow Christ. Yet part of your heavenly focus leads you to give up every part of fleshly living and walk God's spiritual path, as He leads you.

M & M: Ministry and Missions Moment

Just as Jesus fulfilled His part of God's plan by sacrificing everything for you, He expects you to do your part by submitting to His plan for your life. You can do that only if you're willing to give up everything. Decide on one thing you can give up for Him this week. Meditate on the following question: What about the word *everything* do you not understand?

Unit 3

———————— • ————————

PUTTING FEET ON YOUR PRAYERS

Don't you wish you had more energy each day? God has it, and you can tap into it. As God develops you in your inner Spirit, you realize *your point of greatest hurt is the point at which God will bless others beyond your imagination.* He shows you there is a purpose in your suffering, and gives you a different focus for your life. He explodes the old fallacies, opening your spirit to accept unexpected opportunities—the *parentheses*—that interrupt your day. You begin to recognize the "holy coincidences" that stretch your borders.

As He centers your heart-core, He gives you a passion for ministries for which He created you. Filled with His motivation and energy, you begin to understand God's vast imagination and His unbelievable plans for you. Even in tough times, you can break through, expecting God to move—and move you out!

. . . .

If I expect the Lord to move
To make the sin and darkness flee,
Then I must put feet to my prayers
And start the path with energy.
    Wake up! Forget myself, and risk!
    O, God, please change the world through me.

                                  —ee

. . . .

—— Study 11 ——

Moving Out!
God's Energy

One infuriating quality of suffering is that it can immobilize you. If you're living through a hard time, you may be involved in a pity party, overwhelmed by the hard knocks, without time to recover. One mark of depression is inactivity. People with little motivation and energy often sleep all day Saturday and Sunday just to get caught up on their energy for the workday week. You may know people who are caught in a cycle of hurt, unfulfilled dreams, low motivation, and low purpose for their lives.

There's an old saying: You can only walk halfway into a dark forest. After that, you're walking *out of* the dark forest. One sign that you have reached the midpoint of crises and are coming out on the other side is the way you react to life.

Stages of Reaction

If you're walking in the flesh (moving according to the world's rules), you will follow these steps:

1. Something or someone hurts you.
2. You feel pain.
3. You react by attacking the something or someone who hurt you. The attack may be physical or social, passive or active.

If you're walking in the Spirit (moving according to Christ's Spirit

within you), you will follow these steps:
1. Something or someone hurts you.
2. You feel pain.
3. You stop and analyze what Christ would do in the situation.
4. You cool off and make a wise decision, according to the wisdom of Christ.
5. You react by speaking the truth in love (Ephesians 4:15).
6. You forgive, put past differences aside, and move on with serving God in more important pursuits for His Kingdom.
7. You look back on the troubled time as a time of refining.
8. You use what you learned to enrich the lives of others.

Some people like to stay in stage 1 or 2, like Tantalus in Greek mythology, who never learned anything. He stood neck deep in water, yet when he was parched and tried to quench his thirst, the water receded. Large juicy bunches of grapes hung over his head, but when he reached up to eat them, the vine snapped them back, up and away. Our word *tantalize* is derived from *Tantalus*. He was tantalized but never able to move out.

A counselor friend once told me, "For good mental health, move out!" That's the answer to recovery from depression or scarring. Leave past failures, sins, and errors behind as you look forward.

God's Word says, "One thing I do, forgetting those things which are behind and reaching forward to those things which are ahead, I press toward the goal for the prize of the upward call of God in Christ Jesus" (Philippians 3:13–14).

List the three things we should do to reach the high calling of God.

_____

_____

_____

_____

One Step at a Time

God will show you, baby-step-by-baby-step, as your relationship with Him grows. The call from Jesus, "follow Me" is an impetus to move out. A teenager gave me her translation of follow Me: "Get up and move, couch potato! Forget the extra nap and the luxury of watching irrelevant television shows. You're studying your Bible? Don't just study. Act. Don't just sit. Move!"

If you don't know *where to begin* to move out for Christ, start with your family. What can you do to enable your family to follow Christ? Begin by considering their needs. What can you do to meet their needs? What are their skills?

List your family members and their needs.

_____

_____

_____

How can you begin moving forward to meet their needs?

_____

_____

If you're a younger Christian, you may be mystified by God's will. For years I struggled with finding God's will for my life. I received a little light at a time, one step at a time.

Do you ever wonder why a younger Christian, a child in the family, or a brother, or a friend who's a new Christian doesn't get it? The journey with Christ is a mystery.

"We do, however, speak a message of wisdom among the mature. . . . We speak of God's secret wisdom, a wisdom that has been hidden and that God destined for our glory before time began" (1 Corinthians 2:6–7). God hides the wisdom He destined for our glory when we're immature. Only the mature Christians "get it." It takes time to absorb the Spirit of God into our heart's core. God says, "No eye has seen, no ear has heard, no mind has conceived what God has prepared for those who love him. But God has revealed it to us by his Spirit. The Spirit searches all things, even the deep things of God" (1 Corinthians 2:9-10). They're hidden like the Holy of Holies, the Most Holy Place in the tabernacle, behind the veil, or curtain.

"The man without the Spirit does not accept the things that come from the Spirit of God, for they are foolishness to him, and he cannot understand them, because they are spiritually discerned . . . . We have the mind of Christ" (1 Corinthians 2:14, 16*b*). Christ reveals His mind in His time, not ours.

It Takes a Journey

It took you years to learn what you know about Jesus. *It takes the journey of years—before you come even close to spiritual maturity—* understanding God's will for your life. He doesn't just zap us and suddenly we know it all!

My pastor, Kirk Neely, says you'll be *completely mature only after you get to heaven.* Until then, you'll always have "*one more area*" of your heart and life to give Him.

Paul says in Ephesians 3:3 that knowledge of God is "a mystery made known to me by revelation." God says we may "have the full riches of complete understanding, [to] know the mystery of God, namely Christ, in whom are hidden all the treasures of wisdom and knowledge."

God's will is no longer a mystery, as you grow closer to Him. You're willing to accept His will as you deny yourself, take up the cross of Christ, and follow Him. In Ephesians 2:10, Paul says: "We are God's workmanship, created in Christ Jesus to do good works, which God prepared in advance for us to do." God has a work plan for you, as His perfect will for every individual! He says, "Let us not love with words or tongue but with actions and in truth" (1 John 3:18). *As you erase yourself and elevate Christ, the mystery (veil) disappears and you see the face of Jesus!* Spend time getting to know Him. Listen to Him. Ask Him, and He will share with you exactly what He wants you to do.

M & M: Ministry and Missions Moment

You may be one who wants to serve God, but are afraid your energy won't hold out or you'll fail in your service to Him. Remember, God owns all energy and all movement. There's no limit to what God can do. "What is impossible with men is possible with God" (Luke 18:27). Move out, couch potato!

Study 12

Your Hurt, a Help for Others: God's Key

One summer at the Florida Writers Conference in Tampa, a woman came over to the table where we signed our mentoring books and Bible studies. She told about her husband being an abuser. Over the years, he began hitting her. In the middle of one violent confrontation, she left with her two preschoolers in the middle of the night, soon getting a divorce. Years later, when he was ill with AIDS, she nursed him until he died. Unfortunately, after his death, a remarriage caused more chaos for her children, then teenagers. Her son soon joined the army and was killed in Iraq. Her daughter ran away, and this heartbroken mother doesn't know where she is today. Yet she told us something shocking: "I'm so glad I have suffered these things. I wouldn't take a million dollars for the spiritual experiences I've had. I was not a Christian, but during the worst of those days, God spoke to me and became closer than He'd ever been. He hovered over me. I have been filled with such a joy!"

Later another woman came to our book table, telling a similar story about her wayward son. She said, "I know I'm called to help others with those very things I've experienced. I can tell someone how to love a growing child the way God's loved me. No matter what I've done, God still loves me, still loves even my son, who is slowly making a turn. He's showing signs of returning to his faith, and Christian friends are reaching out to him."

Stronger Still

Like these women, I know God's called me to encourage others who are hurting, and *here's an important truth: my point of deepest hurt is the fulcrum point around which my witness can pivot.* My most profound hurts are the very things God uses to encourage others. If I am willing to share them obediently, He can move the world through my obedience. Here are the experiences I share confidentially with those who hurt in these areas: the absence of a military father who left us for two years of active duty (ages 3-5), a sense of insecurity and fear after our house was burglarized (age 6), an unreal sense of ugliness and unworthiness (ages 12–15), downsizing/loss of job (age 22), a miscarriage in the first trimester (age 24), depression from mothering two preschoolers 24/7 (ages 25-31), sudden death of a husband (age 42), single-parenting worries over teenagers who showed signs of grief and ungodliness (ages 43–46), worries over the life-threatening health of adult children (age 52, 54), and death of father (age 56) and mother (age 60). If I were charting my low periods, these would be the "hurt points" of my life. I also complain about inheriting my father's DNA on height, cholesterol, and allergies. Can I encourage someone who's had a miscarriage? Sure. I've been there. Can I encourage a widow? Yes, I know that hurt well. Can I encourage someone whose preschooler died? No, I've never experienced that tragedy. But you, dear reader, may have suffered that hurt, and you can hold the hand of another sister, helping her through that dark valley.

On the chart below, mark your "hurt points."
Birth

_____

_____

Now

As you look back, maybe you think you've had more than your share of trouble. Over the years, however, God has shown me another truth: In His permissive will, He allows you to be exactly who He created you to be: with your DNA and physical, mental, and spiritual heritage. We live in a hazardous, imperfect world. Jesus said, "In this world you will have trouble" (John 16:33). In addition, sin brings opportunity for you to receive its consequences, which always make your life worse. "A man reaps what he sows" (Galatians 6:7). Since all humans have sinned (Romans 3:23), you may have experienced some trouble as a result of sin. Sometimes through our own mistakes, sometimes through the vengeance or carelessness of others, and sometimes through the nature of the world—regardless of where the hurts originate, every life is filled with pleasure and pain, success and disaster, love and hate, good and bad.

What Do You Do with Hurt?

One thing people do with hurt is blame God. However, He never wills bad experiences for you; He never tempts you. He says, "When tempted, no one should say, 'God is tempting me.' For God . . . [does not] tempt anyone" (James 1:13–14). In fact, God says your evil desire conceives and gives birth to sin, and when sin is full-grown, it gives birth to death (James 1:15). When you have succumbed to temptation or are experiencing any trouble, God hovers over you like a good parent, holding you through the crisis, loving you despite your behavior (Proverbs 10:12). He's the perfect giver of gifts to help and encourage you. "Every good and perfect gift is from above, coming down from the Father of the heavenly lights, who does not change like shifting shadows" (James 1:17). He never allows you to experience a crisis to harm you, but to refine your spiritual character, to make you complete in Him. "'For I know the plans I have for you,' declares the Lord, 'plans to prosper you and

not to harm you, plans to give you hope and a future'"
(Jeremiah 29:11).

Read James 1:2-12. List below the suggestions he gives to help you turn trials into triumph.

_____

_____

_____

_____

_____

_____

Your Sharing Key: A Point of Hurt

Once you've been refined as pure silver, passing through the fiery furnace, how can you help others through the same kind of trial? Share your experiences. Once you experienced something, no one can take away your truth. You have a valid testimony to God's goodness through the ups and downs of life. What a treasure! You have the key to solace for other women. A hurting woman will listen to what you say because it rings true. You can tell others the way to survive in chaos is to be *patient in testing and prayerful in trouble*. Using your own life as an example, show her how not just to survive, but to triumph!

Patient in Testing

The most important quality of character that a crisis demands is patience. It's hard to be patient when your life is falling apart. *Trust is a frail commodity during a troubled time.* But because of your own troubles, you can teach the value of patience to a hurting woman. You, like no one else, may be the friend God sends to help her though a dark period. You had to be patient yourself when you went though troubled times, and you can share with her this truth: a sense of trusting Christ carried you through the time of stretched-out patience. You may remind her of Romans 5:2–5: "And we rejoice in the hope of the glory of God. Not only so, but we also rejoice in our sufferings, because we know that suffering produces perseverance; perseverance, character; and character, hope. And hope does not disappoint us, because God has poured out his love into our hearts by the Holy Spirit, whom he has given us." Share with her what the Holy Spirit has meant in your life. (The indwelling Holy Spirit is a difficult concept for some people to comprehend. Only a personal testimony to His presence in your life may make sense to the one with whom you are sharing.) Her life will be changed by your uniqueness. Something about you—just the way God intended for you to be made—may be the key to her trust, growth, and understanding.

Look back at the "hurt points" chart on page 105. Do you know a woman who's experienced the same hurts that you marked on the chart? How can you discern if she needs your encouragement? Watchman Nee says God enables us first to have spiritual understanding as we submit to His will. As a growing Christian, you can somehow sense a spiritual situation in the heart of another woman who gives you clues in her words and actions.

Watch. Listen. Discern. Pray, asking God to make you wise. Once you become sensitive to His Spirit as you interact with a hurting woman, then you'll be able to share words of encouragement. Nee says that once you're fully broken, submitting to His will in daily obedience, you'll be able in a miraculous way to share Christ with others.

Circle the actions below that you could use to bless another.

Join her Bible study group, bowling league, or other activity.

Invite her to your home for tea or coffee.

Ask her family to join yours for a picnic.

Begin a support group for the issue she and you have experienced.

Pray for her.

Ask God to give you wisdom to know what to do.

Prayerful in Trouble

Whether you are hurting during a crisis, or encouraging another person who is hurting, remember God's words: "Is any one of you in trouble? He should pray. . . . The prayer of a righteous man [or woman] is powerful and effective" (James 5:13, 16). Pray with another woman who hurts. In his book, *Be Mature*, Warren Wiersbe says the result of victory over temptation and trials is spiritual maturity. He suggests these four essentials for victory in trials: (1) a joyful attitude; (2) an understanding mind; (3) a surrendered will; and (4) a believing heart. You can share these essentials with another woman as tools for surviving trouble. These four essentials will enable a hurting woman to have an unruffled spirit, regardless of outer circumstances.

Be a Spiritual Thermometer

Watchman Nee says we are *spiritual thermometers*, discerning the spirits of others: (1) first we're patients; (2) next we get healed; (3) then we have the spiritual discernment to recognize the same symptoms in others; and (4) last, we can tell others how to be healed. As we pass these four milestones in our spiritual development, we receive overwhelming blessings from God.

Earlier in this chapter, you charted the "hurt points" in your life. On that same chart, in a different color, chart the "blessed points" (the happiest times of your life). After you've identified the points of blessings in your life, try to identify the *spiritual qualities* that indicate God has blessed you.

Check the qualities below that are true in your life.
- ❑ **Sensitivity to the feelings or hurts of others.**
- ❑ **The spiritual ability to discern others' spiritual condition.**
- ❑ **The physical ability to serve others and encourage them.**
- ❑ **Heartfelt, sincere sympathy/empathy.**
- ❑ **Eternal perspective: all hurts and blessings that come to you are ordered or allowed by God.**
- ❑ **Respect for God and submission to His discipline.**
- ❑ **A sense of blessing that came even from hard times.**
- ❑ **Thankfulness that He's working for your own good, even in your greatest difficulties.**
- ❑ **Peace of heart, whatever the circumstances.**
- ❑ **Calm in time of trial, quiet strength to give others hope.**
- ❑ **Other:**

In retrospect, you can see what God has been doing. You know you can't lead others where you haven't been. Your life and witness are valid only after you have walked through the "valley of the shadow of death" (Psalm 23:4). Your hurt glorifies God as you share His hope with others.

Hannah Hurnard, who wrote *Hinds' Feet on High Places*, also wrote *Mountain of Spices*, in which the king says to Much-Afraid (whose name has been changed to Grace and Glory), "There's absolutely no experience, however terrible, or heartbreaking, or unjust, or cruel, or evil. . . that can harm you if you will but let me teach you how to accept it with joy; and to react to it triumphantly. . . . Every trial, every test, every difficulty. . . through which you may have to pass, is only another opportunity granted to you of conquering an evil thing and bringing out of it something to the lasting praise and glory of God." God will overcome by filling your heart with joy and peace.

M & M: *Ministry and Missions Moment*

Jesus says, "I have told you these things, so that in me you may have peace. . . . Take heart! I have overcome the world" (John 16:33). May you bring glory to God this week as you use your experience as a key to share your inner-heart peace with others.

Use your spiritual thermometer this week to discern someone who has the same hurt you have overcome. Pray for God's wisdom; then help her in the way God leads you.

——— Study 13 ———

Your God-Given Passion: God's Motivation

How can you share your story with others? Perhaps your life is so filled with troubles that you wonder which experiences God wants you to share. Or perhaps your life has been level and calm, without much drama or hurt; you feel you have no story to tell. To determine the direction He wants you to go in the future, explore your past.

As the second oldest grandchild in a group of 19 grandchildren, I was one of the leaders, along with my cousin Lamar. From earliest memory, my grandmother typically asked me to watch the younger children when we had family gatherings. We usually played school, and I was the teacher. Lamar told *Grimm's Fairy Tale* stories, and I taught reading and writing. Sometimes my cousin Peggy showed us how to play roll-a-bat, but I had no interest in the game. I grew up knowing I wanted to be a teacher. In the sixth grade I wrote an essay about how rewarding it would be to teach, and my English teacher loved it! That experience was a milestone in my life. After a few years of wasting time, as teenagers are prone to do, I earned a bachelor's degree in education at a local college and secured a job at the same high school I had attended.

Though I've done other things (store cashier, telephone operator, magazine editor, and writer), I've spent most of my life teaching. One day a fellow teacher said, "Once you start teaching, it's in your blood." I agreed. Teaching had become a passion in my life.

Analyzing Your Passion

The good news is that God puts a passion into every life He creates. You were designed so that your physical health, energy, appearance, and personality; combined with your mental health, intelligence, emotions, and free will—along with your spiritual health, intuition, discernment, wisdom, and prayer-power potential—would accent your passion so that you could serve Christ in the most efficient way. One of God's characteristics is that He doesn't waste anything; He's wasted nothing on you. He's applied and allowed the exact amount of grace, love, discipline, success, and failure that you needed to grow in Him.

As you've grown up, what experiences did God allow that gave you a passion for a certain segment of life? Did a hobby grow into a vocation? Did you have some "holy coincidences" that thrust you into a certain area of your life? As you think of your past, answer the questions below to discover (or rediscover) your passion.

What was your most pivotal turning point? (If you had taken another road, your life would have been entirely different.)

_____

_____

Early in life, what hobby or sport became a passion?

_____

_____

What church activity became a passion?

_____

_____

What personality traits made you perfectly suited for your favorite activities?

_____

_____

What physical characteristics made you perfectly fit for your favorite activities?

_____

_____

As you grew, how did your interests change?

_____

_____

What small, personal choices defined your life?

_____

_____

How did God mature you spiritually through past experiences?

_____

_____

In your daily life, on what activity do you spend the most time?

_____

_____

_____

At this moment, what do you wish you were doing?

_____

_____

What have you habitually dreamed of doing?

_____

_____

What sparked the interest that caused you to dream?

_____

_____

If you had all the money, time, and energy in the world, what would you do?

_____

_____

What or who motivates you?

_____

Analyzing Your Plan

At Pentecost, the disciples heard the sound of a "violent wind that came from heaven and filled the whole house" (Acts 2:2). Immediately after they were filled with the Holy Spirit and began speaking in tongues, a crowd of Jews "from every nation under heaven" gathered because each one heard the Christians speaking in his or her own language. As they listened, they were drawn to God by the power of the Holy Spirit. Today the Holy Spirit still calls people to respond to Him, speaking to them in their own heart languages. Since God created you to be unique—different from anyone else on earth—He calls you uniquely. He offers just the perfect job in His kingdom that fits your body, soul, and spirit. Your past and your passion are integral parts of the total YOU: a perfect fit for the place you have in God's plan. When you have a deep passion for a certain area of ministry, you're motivated to serve Him with all the resources you have.

Review Pain for the Plan

If God is nudging you to serve Him, think of the "hurt points" you related in Study 12. Recall your feelings in the midst of heartache. As you think of your points of deepest hurt, was it at those points you cried out to God, depended on Him only, and stepped into a closer relationship? If so, you have a typical response to God in crisis.

Another of God's characteristics is that He is gentle. He never violates your free will or comes into your heart without an invitation. Only when you ask Him in does He rush to your rescue. And here's an overwhelming principle of His nature: when you get to the point where no one can solve your problem but God, then that's the point at which He sets you free from *all problems*. When His blood washes you clean, it is indiscriminate; He washes away other "hurt points" as well as the immediate one—with grace left over to clean up the corners of your life! (For a further illustration of the cleansing power of the blood, see my book *Friendships of Purpose*, pp. 48–49.) God's power to clean through His presence empowers you to clean up the lives of others with what you learned during a point of trouble or trial. You're now powerful enough to use the point of your pain to help loosen another woman from hers.

Look back at the "blessed points" you wrote on the chart in Study 12. Compare God's blessings to your hurt to see the distance you've come. This might be an outline for your testimony to God's goodness.

Write what you would say to encourage another woman going through a crisis.

I was hurt:

_____

_____

I was blessed:

_____

_____

God has changed my life:

_____

_____

Spend Time with God

Before you step out in faith to help someone else, spend time at church, in Bible study, and in prayer. The psalmist says, "One thing I ask of the Lord, this is what I seek: that I may dwell in the house of the Lord all the days of my life, to gaze upon the beauty of the Lord and to seek him in his temple. For in the day of trouble he will keep me safe in his dwelling. He will hide me in the shelter of his tabernacle" (Psalm 27:4–5). Sometimes God speaks to you more powerfully as you worship Him in His tabernacle, your local church, where you hear different perspectives of His work in you.

As you praise Him, seek God with all your heart. "Hear my voice when I call, O Lord. . . . Your face, Lord, I will seek" (Psalm 27:7–8). Read God's Word, and ask God to guide you. "Show me your ways, O Lord; teach me your paths; guide me in our truth and teach me. . . and my hope is in you all day long" (Psalm 25:4–5). Memorize Scriptures you can share with another woman. "I have hidden your word in my heart that I might not sin against you" (Psalm 119:11).

Follow God's Plan

To serve God, don't get ahead of Him. If you want to share your story with someone else, ask Him to show you *His* plan, don't ask Him to help you with *yours*. "In his heart a man plans his course, but the Lord determines his steps" (Proverbs 16:9). He will help you share with a group—perhaps a support group for those involved in a certain issue—or with an individual. Lay your passion on the altar; ask God to take your experience with hurts and blessings and offer them to others for their good.

Customize Your Plan

As you prepare, find Bible verses that you might give (on a card, email note, or decorated/matted and framed). Under which condition or conflict might you use each of the following to encourage another woman?

- "Who may ascend the hill of the Lord? Who may stand in his holy place? He who has clean hands and a pure heart" (Psalm 24:3-4).
- "When you lie down, you will not be afraid . . . for the Lord will be your confidence" (Proverbs 3:26).
- "Pleasant words are a honeycomb, sweet to the soul and healing to the bones" (Proverbs 16:24).
- "Put to death . . . sexual immorality, impurity, lust, evil desires and greed" (Colossians 3:5).
- "Rid yourselves of all such things as these: anger, rage, malice, slander, and filthy language from your lips" (Colossians 3:8).
- "Do not lie to each other" (Colossians 3:9).

- "Respect those who work hard among you, who are over you in the Lord and who admonish you" (1 Thessalonians 5:12).
- "God is just: He will pay back trouble to those who trouble you and give relief to you who are troubled" (2 Thessalonians 1:6-7).
- "Love your neighbor" (Matthew 5:43).
- "Love your enemies" (Matthew 5:44).
- "Pray for those who persecute you" (Matthew 5:44).
- "I urge. . . that requests, prayers, intercession and thanksgiving be made for everyone—for kings and all those in authority" (1 Timothy 2:1–2).
- "Guard what has been entrusted to your care. Turn away from godless chatter and the opposing ideas of what is falsely called knowledge" (1 Timothy 6:20).

You may use each of these verses in a variety of situations. One miraculous truth about God's Word is that it comes alive as a person reads it, applying it to every situation.

M & M: Ministry and Missions Moment

God says, "There is a way that seems right to a man, but in the end it leads to death" (Proverbs 14:12). Don't make decisions in any plan without the Master leading. Get advice from other godly Christians this week to help analyze your plan and pray for you as you share. "Plans fail for lack of counsel, but with many advisers they succeed" (Proverbs 15:22).

As you go, keep your eyes on Jesus, "being confident of this, that he who began a good work in you will carry it on to completion until the day of Christ Jesus."

——— Study 14 ———

Unexpected Opportunities: God's Borders

If God is the Master of the universe, as we said in Study 1, then He's in control, right? If that is so, then why doesn't He take charge of everything? Why do unexpected things happen? Your car breaks down. You get lost. You lock yourself out of the house. A car wreck kills your loved one.

You misspell a word you know how to spell—and it is printed in the church newsletter. You plan for weeks, and then forget to follow through on the day you planned. And what about the times you planned for two children and had four? And the time you planned an outdoor wedding and it rained buckets? We live in a world of the unexpected.

Last year I planned to fly from Greenville, South Carolina, to Sacramento. Two other speakers—Cherie Nettles and Kimberly Sowell—rode on the same flight. We were disgruntled to find that I was slated for a middle seat across the aisle from them. Since we had drama and messages to practice, we asked a man to swap seats, but he laughed and refused to sit between the two other women passengers beside me. Resigned to our fate, Cherie and Kimberly had a great time chatting and studying while I sat between two strangers, who introduced themselves as an Egyptian housewife and a German-born survivor of the holocaust. To be honest, it took me a few minutes before I figured out God had placed me there to witness to a Jew and a Muslim. Before I could turn the conversation to Jesus, the German woman, Hulda, asked, "Have you been born again?" Stunned, I uttered some intelligent remark, such as "Duh. . . . Oh, uh. . . ." Before she heard my response, she said, "I heard Jimmy Carter say he'd been born again in 1975, and I've wondered about it ever since."

I caught up with God at that point, and tried to wake up to His Spirit's leading. "Yes, I've been born again," I responded. "Would you like me to tell you about the day it happened to me?"

"Yes. I'd like to hear it."

I told her about going to Vacation Bible School one hot summer when I was a preteen, learning about Romans 3:23 and Romans 8:1–4, 28; and playing softball in the churchyard. I went home dusty and sweaty as the soft dust dried in small lines on my legs. That night mother did something unusual. She let my brother Jim and me go to bed without a bath! What a delicious privilege! I jumped happily into bed . . . until it began to feel gritty. I then remembered what a young man had said to me at church: that I needed God and He needed me. I wondered why the Almighty God who hung the moon and set the stars in place could possibly need me. I was ignorant, young, and dirty. I looked at my dried-dusty legs. Yet God needed me—He wanted a relationship with ME! Suddenly I realized I was dirty inside as well as outside. That young man said all of us had sinned and fallen short of the glory of God. I realized I had a lot of sin on my heart that night. For one thing, I'd knocked Jim's front teeth out with a softball—on purpose. And I hadn't been sorry, either. For another thing, I'd pinched my cousin Lamar's upper arm until it turned blue—because he wanted to play with someone else. I realized for the first time I'd been a mean girl who ought to know better. Sensing His presence in my room, I said, "God, I can't imagine what You'd need with a skinny, dirty girl like me. I don't have anything to give You; but, Lord, right now, I want to give You everything I am and everything I ever will be. I don't want to be a mean girl. I'm sorry. I want You to help me live the way *You* want me to live."

The moment I spoke, I felt my world change. He filled me with a great sense of happiness and deep-down peace. I felt clean. I was born again in the Spirit, and I've never been the same since. I've known Jesus now for over 50 years, and He gets better every day!

When I finished sharing my born-again experience, I looked to my right and the Egyptian, Fattan was weeping. "Fattan," I said, "have you been born again?"

"Yes," she said. I nearly fell out of my seat.

"Uh, would you like to tell Hulda how it happened?" I asked.

Fattan told her story of being a Presbyterian pastor's daughter—not a Muslim, as I had assumed! Her conversion was different from mine, but she told of a step-by-step process that led to the night she realized she had been born again through a spiritual rebirth. She also confirmed the presence of God in her reborn heart every day.

No, Hulda, my new German friend, wasn't reborn on the airplane to Sacramento, though Fattan and I both offered Scriptures and gave her the opportunity. Both of us trust God to send another Christian into her life to water the seed we planted.

Do we believe it was accidental that I had to sit across the aisle from my speaker-friends? Not at all. Christians don't believe in accidents. We believe in God-appointed holy coincidences. I have no doubt God sent Hulda and Fattan to sit in those divine-appointed seats, and He sent me to sit in the middle.

Oswald Chambers calls such a moment a "parenthesis" that flows into your life. As a maturing Christian, look out for the parentheses in your life. What some people may call accidents, you can recognize as the hand of God. When something unusual happens, look around you. Catch up with God's Spirit as He nudges you to use the parentheses as opportunities to witness.

"Connie," a singer in a trio, once began a two-hour drive to sing at a statewide Christian women's meeting. On the way, the car stalled. Getting out, the three women flagged down a highway patrolman, who called a wrecker, which towed them to a garage. Of course, their first thought was that God had prevented an important opportunity for them to sing. They prayed and begged God to give them back their opportunity and make the repairs quick. Time passed as they waited, and they realized they'd missed the pre-meeting banquet. They shared a pack of crackers out of the repair shop's machine. As they munched, they watched other employees go home, leaving only one mechanic, who worked on their engine. However, he stopped working on the car and began to tell them about his troubles. Two women in the trio became frustrated and angry, but the third cared about his problems. She shared a similar trouble in her life. Before long, she had led him to ask Jesus into his heart, to give him peace about his situation.

As soon as the engine was repaired, the trio left, celebrating the salvation of the mechanic, understanding why they needed to be there. They arrived at the meeting in time to rush to the podium and sing, "How Great Thou Art." The trio had experienced a parenthesis that had flowed into the middle of their journey.

Have you ever experienced a parenthesis in your day? Write the story here:

_____

_____

_____

_____

_____

A Parenthesis in the First Century

After Pentecost, great persecution erupted against the church at Jerusalem and some Christians left town. Philip went to Samaria to preach the gospel (Acts 8:1–8). Simon, a magician in Samaria, became a Christian after Philip shared with him about Jesus. God then sent Philip down the south road toward Gaza, where he encountered an Ethiopian who was reading the Old Testament book of Isaiah.

Read the following verses from Acts 8 and match the lettered verses to the numbered sentences below them, indicating Christian actions.

a. Verse 26: "Now an angel of the Lord said to Philip, 'Go south to the road—the desert road—that goes down from Jerusalem to Gaza.'"

b. Verse 27a: "So he started out. . . ."

c. Verse 27b-28: "he met an Ethiopian eunuch. . . . reading the book of Isaiah."

d. Verse 29: "The Spirit told Philip, 'Go to that chariot and stay near it.'"

e. Verse 30: "Then Philip ran up to the chariot. . . . 'Do you understand what you are reading?' Philip asked."

f. Verse 35: "Then Philip began with that very passage of Scripture and told him the good news about Jesus."

g. Verse 36-38: "As they traveled. . . the eunuch said, 'Look, here is water. Why shouldn't I be baptized?'. . . and Philip baptized him."

h. Verse 39 "The eunuch. . . . went on his way rejoicing."

Place the letters above in the appropriate blank:

_____ 1. A parenthesis just happened to interrupt a Christian's journey when he saw a stranger reading the Bible.

_____ 2. After the Christian had told the stranger the good news about Jesus, the stranger wanted to confirm that He was a believer.

_____ 3. A Christian responded and went on a trip.

_____ 4. An angel led a Christian to a parenthesis in his life.

_____ 5. A Christian was able to share the plan of salvation.

_____ 6. A Christian's witness during an "accidental encounter" gave joy to another man.

_____ 7. The Holy Spirit nudged a Christian to witness to a stranger.

_____ 8. A believer responded to the Holy Spirit and offered to share with a non-believer and teach God's Word.

Answers: 1-c, 2-g, 3-b, 4-a, 5-f, 6-h, 7-d, 8-e.

Enlarging Your Territory

Like Philip, you recognize opportunities that flow into your everyday life. The challenge for a Christian comes at the point you recognize the parenthesis-pause in your plans. A serious Christian—that is, one who acknowledges Jesus as her Master—will never fail to respond. She recognizes God's call, reacting instantly. She doesn't delay; she doesn't look at her watch. She doesn't think of other, more important things because she knows God's work *is* the most important thing.

New Borders to Your Witness

Through a variety of circumstances, first-century Christians told their world about Christ. Their witness caused fights in the streets, beatings, and incarceration. At times they wisely left town before they were persecuted so they could share the gospel again. As they traveled, they enlarged their witnessing territory and were able to tell about Christ and His hope for the world in many homes, to individuals and crowds. First-century Christians moved from Jerusalem to Samaria, Galilee, Syria, Asia Minor (now Turkey), and other areas, eventually moving to Italy, the rest of Europe, northern Africa, and finally to America and other parts of the world. By the fourth century, the entire Roman Empire had been declared Christian!

Today's American lives in a transient society. If you don't move, then sometimes the world moves to your community. Stop now and think of your mobility. How has your witnessing territory been enlarged? Are you in a new territory now, hesitating to give a bold witness?

Fill in the circles below, listing things you've done to witness as you moved from the town in which you were born to the town where you live now. List other places you've once visited or lived. If you ministered and/or witnessed in those places, mark with an asterisk and note in the margin what you did there. Think of what you've done to reach your world for Christ. Then consider what you have *not* done. Your missionary movement is no less important than that of the first-century Christians; God gives each Christian the ability to move people in her world closer to Him, as she's willing to let Him lead her.

Today may be the day God shows you a new ministry area.

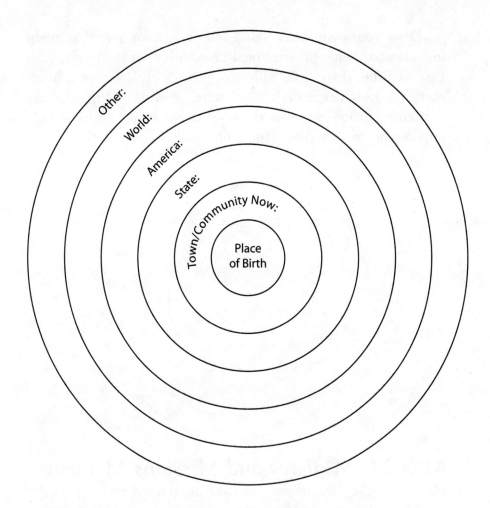

Other:
World:
America:
State:
Town/Community Now:
Place of Birth

Changes Resulting from Your Witness

Do you notice in the concentric circles above that you are concentrating on one area? For instance, your Christian witness has
taken place within your own community? Are you sure God has
called you to that area? If so, you're fulfilling His will for your
life. However, if you see other areas you know need a witness
but you've never gone there, pray, asking God to show you how
and where He wants you to serve Him.

Draw your own concentric circles as shown here that might include your home (a devotional time with your husband), your yard (a Bible story time with a neighbor's children, or a block party for new neighbors), your state (a mission trip to share Scripture portions at a resort), or overseas (make crafts to help missionaries with a Bible school on another continent).

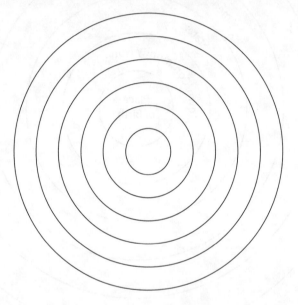

M & M: *Ministry and Missions Moment*

How about the parentheses that have interrupted your days in the past? How did you turn those flat tires, blizzards, or other circumstances into opportunities to share Christ with others? If you didn't think ahead, remember, it's never too late to plan with God. Begin this week by learning how to tell God's plan of salvation to someone else. (Your pastor or women's leader can give you suggestions).

Copy and learn how to use the Scripture references in Study 13. Have them handy as you go. Then ask God to give you discernment to be aware of His flowing a parenthesis into your life that causes you to pause and open up time for a witness to His love.

——— Study 15 ———

"Mystery Jobs" Outside the Church: God's Imagination

In times of trouble, the watermark of a spiritually mature Christian is that she'll follow God to the ends of the earth. Where are you willing to serve? God may not intend for you to work just in your local church or to set a good example only in your home. He may ask you to move out in a mission trip. Linda Gilden, a talented speaker and author of *Love Notes on His Pillow*, tells about the diverse jobs she found on a mission trip.

"Sometimes the greatest challenges are the logistics of a mission trip rather than the mission itself! For more than 38 years, my church has sponsored a mission trip for the youth of the church every summer. I went on the first trip as a high school student. Now I am proudly known as the head 'Mountain Mama!'

"Eight years ago, a new youth minister came to our church. Realizing this trip could be a little overwhelming, I offered to help coordinate the crafts for the 1,500 children and youth we would have in Vacation Bible School that week in the hills of Kentucky. My little God-picked team of four quickly became known as the Mountain Mamas.

"From the very first group of 30 youth and adults traveling in personal cars, we have grown to more than 250 youth and adults on a team that travels in 26 large vans, 8 minivans, several pickup trucks, and two 18-wheelers.

"Our craft assignment quickly grew. Before leaving home, we enlisted senior citizens to cut and count. GA (Girls in Action) groups helped ready materials and make sample crafts. Not only did we prepare the materials and sort them for each van of youth missionaries to pick up on their way into the hills and hollers, we began to do other jobs. We tended the sick and delivered mail. We made peanut butter sandwiches and fruit smoothies every afternoon for snacks. A year or two later, our youth minister decided to provide T-shirts for every participant. They would have three identical shirts of different colors. Obviously, three shirts were not enough to work hard outdoors all day for a week.

"So the Mountain Mamas became laundresses, washing around 500 T-shirts each day. As we removed each one and folded it on top of the dryer, we prayed for the owner of the shirt by name. This gave the Mountain Mamas a real sense of involvement in the Bible Schools as we called each person by name. (We also kept up with who did not have enough shirts in the wash and needed to be reminded to change!)

"One of the precedents established early in the career of the Mountain Mamas was providing 'van surprises' for the kids on the way down the mountain. We tried to think of something to put on the vans to say to the kids one more time, 'We love you and think you're special.' M&M's had risen to the top as the treat of choice for the Mountain Mamas.

"One year was especially busy. We didn't have time to shop. 'What are we going to do?' asked Sheila. 'There is no time to shop for van surprises.'

"On Thursday before our Saturday departure, a deacon in a nearby church invited the Mountain Mamas out to lunch. We enjoyed a nice visit with him and his family.

"As we were walking out the door, he said, 'I have something I'd like to give the kids. Opening the trunk of his car he continued,

'I have a candy business. Here are 300 packs of M&M's.'

"That year the kids received their van surprises along with the story of how God provided them. God cares about us when we pour ourselves out for Him. God gives us the strength to persevere and answers our prayers for confidence when we're out of our comfort zones. God cares that we have clean T-shirts and healthy snacks. And, yes, God even cares about van surprises!"

Scattered Around the World

The troubling lack of the Mountain Mamas gave God the opportunity to provide surprises. God must have given the first-century Christians surprises, also, as they witnessed to others in strange places. The apostle Peter wrote two extant letters to Christians who had been scattered throughout the Roman world. He calls them "strangers in the world" (1 Peter 1:1), because they were refugees, misplaced because of their faith in Christ. God may be calling you to be a refugee, a stranger, or a Mountain Mama washing T-shirts, but you've been dragging your feet because of your comfort at home. He may need to light a fire under you.

Trouble as Fire, to Get You to Move

I grew up in a small town, with never a thought of moving away. I married the boy next door, who had a job in town, and we reared two children in the local schools, in fellowship with a local church. Two years after my husband died, I experienced a broken engagement. It seems that every time I went out of the house, I ran into my former fiancé, who sometimes walked arm-in-arm with a variety of beautiful women. For a few years I wondered why God allowed me to experience the hurt of a broken engagement and subsequent loss of direction for my life. The whole experience puzzled me. Then one day I understood.

While teaching school, I was called to the office. I answered the "very important phone call," as the school secretary had said, and found, to my surprise, a job offer to become the editor of a national Christian women's magazine, *Royal Service*. I had read that magazine for years and was honored to be asked. I prayed very briefly, asked my pastor's advice, and took the job. Years later someone asked, "How did you have the courage to leave your parents and two children in college here in South Carolina, and go to a state 400 miles away where you knew no one? I then realized that one of the factors that made me leave the comfort of home was the broken engagement. It was pleasant to make a new start, without running into anyone who caused unpleasant memories. I firmly believe that God allowed the broken engagement to encourage me to move out! Otherwise I may never have gone. God had to light a fire under me to get me to move!

I share with other mothers that one reason I believe teenagers cause so much friction in their families is that *they must have great discontent* at home to grow the courage to move out. Before they leave for college or career, they need some uncomfortable impetus to make them leave the only home they've ever known. Disgruntlement and confrontation with parents and siblings (and a few puppy-love broken hearts) are a preparation for independence.

Mary Ann Appling once wrote, "It is hard to leave people who seem just like you. Yet, sometimes God asks you to do that."

Have you ever been on a mission trip like the Mountain Mamas and their youth? What happened?

_____

_____

_____

_____

Have you had clues (troubles, discomfort, wanderlust) that God may be asking you to move out? Explain.

_____

_____

Which people who aren't like you is God nudging you to love?

_____

_____

_____

Pray. Then write what He's asking you to do now.

_____

_____

_____

_____

Trouble as Preparation for God's Work

If you're experiencing trouble or trial in your present situation, God may be preparing you for an independence from your place of past comfort. Many people give the testimony of critical supervisors or a cantankerous co-worker that caused them to quit an unfulfilling job, only to find a new one with more money, more benefits, and much more fulfillment. A woman I admire, Karen McGuire, once shared this classic quote with me, "God never closes a door without opening a window." I watched her example as she took several windows of opportunity, as God led her. In *Risk the Journey*, Bill Leonard said, "Faith is a risk, pure and simple." Helen Fling said,

"There is always risk in change. But there is greater risk in standing still."

Trouble as Wisdom for the Future

Trouble always teaches us wisdom. It is only in suffering that we learn. (I've always wished the reverse were true. I don't like to admit it hurts to change and grow in God.) When you go through a period of hurt and suffering, or a period of fear and trembling, be assured you'll move out in strength, assurance, and powerful resolve. The wisdom God teaches you through suffering is a survival tool no one can take away from you. The inner resources you've gained from Him will allow you to face anything with confidence!

_____

_____

_____

List spiritual resources God has given you.

_____

_____

_____

_____

M & M: Ministry and Missions Moment

God's energy is exciting when you latch on to it. His imagination never limits you. It's only yours that holds you back.

How far are you willing to go? Call someone in your church about going on a mission trip like the one the Mountain Mamas complete each summer. Sign up this week!

Unit 4

———— • ————

FINDING STRENGTH
IN HIS WORD

Now it's time to get practical. You've experienced heartbreaking trials, tests, and troubles; you've learned from the hard knocks of life. You *know* God. Though you've acknowledged God's Word as eternal truth for a long time, this Advent moment is the time to try His strength. Absorb the wisdom of His words only to a certain point. Then put them into practice. Express the mind of Christ to the world!

How long has it been since you have moved out of your comfort zone? No service for Christ is valid if it's stagnant. He intends for the seeds of truth in His Word to be scattered across the face of the earth. Find out how His plan for the world relates to your own God-designed ministry of the Word. Whether it's individual, a two-by-two Bible study with a dear friend, or a group dynamic, go deeper into the Word of the Lord. Then display what He's taught you in your microcosm—and beyond. God will bless your ministry, word for word, word by word, in worldwide seed scattering.

. . . .

O Lord, how wise and great you are;
With messages of love for me.
Through pearls of wisdom strengthen all;
Display your Word, to set us free.
    Help me to lead my dear loved ones
    Who look for God's eternity.

—ee

. . . .

────── Study 16 ──────

The Wisdom of Scripture

If the tough times of life serve as warnings that you need to strengthen your relationship with Him and think of outside possibilities, then what do you do after the tough times are over? After you've delved into the mind of God and understand Him better, how does that change your life?

No doubt you'll be a wiser woman, more comfortable in a godly environment, and able to express the mind of Christ to the world. And what about your actions, as you use your wisdom?

The Impossible Principle

Because of your experience and that of others around you, you can apply what you've learned to everyday life, making it more abundant, rich in grace. I believe in a phenomenon I call the "impossible principle": *Jesus always calls the most reluctant to do something He knows they can't do in their own power*, as He proves He's Sovereign Lord.

Sherry Gessner of Virginia Beach, Virginia, tells a wonderful story of how she was led by "the hand of God." Years ago, Sherry wondered what she could find on the computer about Jesus and His people. She typed in JESUS AND JEWS. Among the assorted sites was Jews for Jesus. Who would know more about Jesus, she thought, than the Jews? When she read their newsletter, she realized these "completed Jews," who believed in Jesus, had outstanding boldness in sharing His love with other Jews who didn't know Him. She says,

"I felt a tug on my heart when I remembered the Lord's command to spread the gospel to all parts of the world, starting in Judea (the Jews' homeland). One day I read their offer to join them in street evangelism in Washington, D.C. I didn't think they would accept my application, but a year later I got a congratulations letter in the mail. I remember saying, 'Who me? You got to be crazy, Lord. I can't do this.' Then a still, small voice said. 'You can't, but I can.' I can say that every time I go I've gotten stronger and bolder. I sometimes laugh. Imagine me, the coward who couldn't witness. Jesus made me rejoice in my infirmities."

Sherry hasn't found it easy to witness to non-Christians in Washington. Financially it's not always convenient. She says God always moves her on her way. "I usually send out thank-you notes to those who help pay my expenses. One gentleman thanked me for the note and sent a $20 bill. I was on my way for the next trip. I just stopped when the money fell out and said, 'Yes, Lord. Me. Again? I'm off on another mission trip!' He always provides."

God says, "'Come, all you who are thirsty, come to the waters; and you who have no money, come, buy and eat! . . . Listen, listen to me, and eat what is good, and your soul will delight in the richest of fare. Give ear and come to me; hear me, that your soul may live'. . . . Seek the Lord while he may be found; call on him while he is near. . . . 'For my thoughts are not your thoughts, neither are your ways my ways,'" declares the Lord. 'As the heavens are higher than the earth, so are my ways higher than your ways and my thoughts than your thoughts'" (Isaiah 55:1, 2b-3, 6, 8-9).

Have you ever experienced the impossible principle? Explain.

_____

_____

_____

Write in your own words what **Listen to me, and eat what is good** mean to you.

_____

_____

God says, "Seek the Lord while he may be found." When can the Lord be found?

_____

_____

Where can He be found?

_____

_____

Sherry and many other women like her have learned from Scriptures such as the one above the following truths:

1. We can come to God anytime, anywhere. He's our total resource.
2. God fills our hunger and thirst for spirituality.
3. Even when we have few resources, God provides.
4. God is near.
5. God's ways are amazing, far above ours, yet He's always willing to give wisdom.
6. God gives us wisdom through His Word.

In the Beginning, God's Word

Most Christians know that God's Word has power; yet, we're constantly surprised when it alone changes hearts. God says, "In the beginning was the Word, and the Word was with God and the Word was God" (John 1:1–2). John is speaking of the Logos, Greek for "word," but He capitalizes it because this Word is a person: Jesus is our Logos, our Word. It is not accidental that Christ is called the Word. God chose the spoken word to accomplish gigantic feats. The first chapter of Genesis is filled with "And God said 'Let there be. . . . And it was so." Just think: Creation was accomplished through the spoken word!

Nothing Became Something

God "made the heavens by the word of his command" (2 Peter 3:5 NLT). He spoke over *nothing* and it became *something*. The psalmist says, "The Lord thundered from heaven; the voice of the Most High resounded" (Psalm 18:13). The prophets of the Old Testaments repeated, "Thus saith the Lord." In the gospels alone, you will find "Jesus said" hundreds of times. After Pentecost you will find "The Holy Spirit said" (Acts 13:2).

Second Generation Words

One of God's plans for the world was that humans could speak, read, and write. These skills were important for communicating God's presence in the lives of His children. God even asked His people to wear His words on phylacteries (leather boxes) as a "reminder on your forehead that the law of the Lord is to be on your lips" (Exodus 13:9 and Deuteronomy 6:4–9). They faithfully shared God's Word with the next generation. From the first century until now, the apostles and other Christians have recorded God's second-generation words (Matthew 23:5). John says, "Then he said, 'Write this down, for these words are trustworthy and true'" (Revelation 21:5).

God's Language: Metaphors of Life

God's words reflect His rich abundance. It's remarkable to me that God's words aren't just practical and factual, but they resound with lush eloquence. Years ago a Bible teacher told me God's Word is a giant metaphor (a *comparison* with rich symbolism.).

You can use the following metaphors from John to tell about Jesus: "I am the bread of life" (6:35); "I am the light of the world" (8:12); "I am the gate" (10:7); "I am the good shepherd" (10:14); "I am the resurrection and the life" (11:25); "I am the way, the truth, and the life" (14:6); "I am the vine; you are the branches" (15:5).

What metaphors explain who God is in your life? List in your own words who God is, following the examples below.

God is love.

God is a raindrop, gently growing and nourishing me.

_____

_____

_____

_____

God's Word is pervasive. It still thunders today. If you allow it to enter your heart, then basic godly living will be the result of God's Word in you. You'll hear it everywhere; you even hear it in silence. In quiet moments, His strong words can be heard clearly!

Futile Mind or Fertile Mind?

Paul says, "I tell you this, and insist on it in the Lord, that you must no longer live as the Gentiles do, in the futility of their thinking" (Ephesians 4:17). A futile mind leads to depression, despair, and hopelessness. When you're separated from God because of ignorance of His Word, He says you may "indulge in every kind of impurity with a continual lust for more" (Ephesians 4:19).

What a difference when you internalize Scripture! Your futile mind becomes a fertile one. God says, "As the rain and the snow come down from heaven and do not return to it without watering the earth and making it bud and flourish. . . so is my word that goes out from my mouth: It will not return to me empty, but will accomplish what I desire and achieve the purpose for which I sent it" (Isaiah 55:10–11). Since your Creator is creative, your mind will be energized, flourishing, active, hopeful; it becomes fertile, not futile.

Read Ephesians 4:25 to 5:7. List instructions for a life of wisdom.

_____

_____

_____

_____

_____

_____

_____

"Be very careful, then, how you live—not as unwise but as wise, making the most of every opportunity, because the days are evil. Therefore do not be foolish, but understand what the Lord's will is" (Ephesians 5:15).

You can listen in church, where we find the _depths_ of God. There you find preachers of the Word, Bible teachers with depth of insight, and other Christians who share their experience with the wisdom of Scripture. More importantly, you will experience the presence of Christ in church and wherever you go. Pay attention!

Listen to Him. "You have seen many things, but have paid no attention. . . . Which of you will listen to this or pay close attention in time to come?" (Isaiah 42:20, 23).

A Willing Mind

Once you know, you can share God's will and wisdom: "Be wise in the way you act toward outsiders; make the most of every opportunity. Let your conversation be always full of grace, seasoned with salt, so that you may know how to answer everyone" (Colossians 4:5–6). David said to his son Solomon, "Acknowledge the God of your father, and serve him with wholehearted devotion and with a willing mind" (1 Chronicles 28:9).

What do Christians do? "We proclaim him, admonishing and teaching everyone with all wisdom. . . . with all his energy, which so powerfully works in me" (Colossians 1:28–29).

Remember God's economic principle: He never wastes anything on you. Verses you learned as a child are resources to serve you in adulthood. If you are a Christian, yielded to God's will, then He'll provide opportunities to use His Holy Word from years ago, recently, or today. He wants you to fulfill His will by using the Scriptures.

Right now, pause a moment and recall verses of Scripture you learned as a child. Which words were likely to have been absorbed in your mind even before you could express them to others? If any come to mind, write them here.

_____

_____

_____

_____

_____

_____

_____

_____

Fill Your Spirit

I cannot emphasize enough the power of the Word of Christ as it grows in usage and influence over the years. Put verses to memory every day, and they will return at appropriate times, as God leads you to share Him with others.

For more about God's Word and the mind of Christ read *Deeper Still: A Woman's Study to a Closer Walk with God*, Study 4.

M & M: Ministry and Missions Moment

When people think sharing the Word is too hard, and complain, "I can't do it," God says, "The word is very near you; it is in your mouth and in your heart so you may obey it" (Deuteronomy 30:14). Start today to obey God's command: "Always prepare to give an answer to everyone who asks you to give the reason for the hope that you have" (1 Peter 3:15). Memorize Scriptures in this study this week.

——— Study 17 ———

Ministering Through Scripture

I don't know anyone who exemplifies Christian ministering through Scripture better than Gene and Ann Ellis. Their answering machine begins with the words, "For God so loved the world." At the end of John 3:16, the usual words welcome the call, asking the caller to leave a number. Gene and Ann are dedicated servant leaders in my church in Spartanburg. They are quick to give Scriptures to encourage other church members, but their greatest work is witnessing to non-church members: the homeless; internationals; and needy people of all language groups.

For many years the Ellises taught English as a Second Language (ESL) to internationals in Florida. Ann says, "One major attraction to our ministry was Bibles in their heart languages for students to take home. Each week we sang the theme song, 'Love in Any Language.' In less than nine years we served over 600 internationals from 61 countries. Several internationals made professions of faith. Picnics, the church's Christmas pageants, and field trips to local attractions were vital in reaching extended family members and friends." Their ministry began to spread out in widening circles.

"Lia Temple, a mature Christian from Brazil, attended the first class. She was a student at Brevard Community College who had been deeply burdened for the international students there. When she heard about our ministry, she said it was an answer to prayer. She eventually started a Portuguese Bible study and reached out to the Portuguese-speaking community. Several students accepted Christ."

One Russian couple, Val and Nina Jerova, once students at Moscow University, enrolled in the classes, but didn't come back until a year later. At that time, they told their story. While living in Russia, they realized their country was about to open up to foreign visitors. Val obtained a plane, hired a pilot, and started a tour business.

When Val learned about what it meant to be a Christian, he wanted to be one. Ann says, "While in the CE (Conversational English) class, he asked a million questions. Then he experienced for himself being born again and baptized. Later Val and Nina were convinced they needed to return to Russia on several mission trips to share Christ with their own people. They even started a seminary correspondence course." God's Word was still spreading.

Ann and Gene made sure all internationals took Scripture with them when they came and went. At events like the "everybody's birthday party," Ann often gave her testimony: "My father was a pastor, and I had been in church all my life; I knew many Bible stories and had a head knowledge about Christianity. When I was 13, I heard the famous evangelist, Billy Graham. At that time I truly understood what it meant to be a Christian and that I needed to repent from my sin and ask Jesus to become my Savior. That was my spiritual birth. I then had a physical birthday and a spiritual birthday." Then Ann gave each international a card explaining what *born again* meant.

Maria de Pereyra from Argentina took her card home one night after the birthday party, read it on her own, and prayed to receive Christ into her heart. Several months later, her family (husband, Jorge; Jorge Jr.; and Maria Jr.) ate dinner at Ann and Gene's home. While eating, Maria said, "Ann, tell Maria Jr. about your birthdays." She did, and Maria Jr. prayed to receive Christ into her heart.

The widening circle continued as the family moved back to Argentina, encouraging other incoming Argentines to seek out CE lessons at a Christian church. Ann and Gene take joy in knowing that students who've learned English in the United States are sharing Jesus in many areas of the world.

The best was yet to come. In January 2000, the Ellises met a young Turkish woman, Husniye, at an ESL reception. That fall, Turkey was the focus of their church's International Mission Study. During this emphasis, as they prayed for Turkey, God brought Turkey to them in the form of Husniye, who resurfaced as a "holy coincidence" from God.

Today as the relationship has developed, Husniye considers the Ellises her stateside parents. Ann says, "We've also 'adopted' her as our daughter. In 2006 it was an honor to be invited to visit Turkey with her and meet her parents, brother, and sister, and their families. As a guest in their home in Izmir (Smyrna in Bible times), we were warmly welcomed and treated with kindness and love."

During the trip the Ellises went on a two-week/2,200-mile bus tour of Turkey, visiting Ephesus, Colosse, and Galatia. They prayed that the Lord would open the door for a witness in the 99 percent-Muslim country, and He did. Husniye's brother and sister asked questions about Christianity, and the Ellises shared Scripture, trusting that one day it will bear fruit. God also answered their prayers on the bus tour. While explaining the custom of burying the dead facing Mecca so that in the resurrection they will rise up and be born again, the tour guide turned to the Ellises and asked, "What do you believe about being born again?" Ann gave a brief explanation to everyone. Later a young woman from Australia asked if they were born again. Gene and Ann both shared their testimonies and gave her a Bible. They also were able to witness to a Muslim dental student on the plane back to Izmir, giving him a tract. Wherever they go, to the other side of the world or next door, Ann and Gene Ellis share God's Word.

Great Things for God

In his book, *Knowing God*, J. I. Packer lists these four evidences that you know God:

1. **You have great energy for God.** Some people in our church get tired just following the Ellises around. In spite of cataract surgery and knee replacement, they outstrip many younger members in ministry. Daniel, a captive in Babylonia, was a good example of a young man who did great things for God. He and fellow captives Shadrach, Meshach, and Abednego refused the rich food and wine of Babylonian royalty, and instead were filled with robust health and energy from vegetables and water (Daniel 1:11-20). God gives special excitement, enthusiasm, and energy as you follow Him.

2. **You have great thoughts of God.** When Husniye first invited the Ellises to go to Turkey, they didn't hesitate. Always optimistic, they changed their busy calendar and bought tickets for the witnessing opportunity of a lifetime. Ann laughed, saying, "Husniye is spending our money as if she were our real child," and then plunged ahead into God's plans. From a study of God's Word, He gives mental acumen and understanding (Daniel 1:17–20). Discipline yourself to study God's Word daily, and you will "take the high road" of optimistic thought, as Daniel did.

3. **You show great boldness for God.** Though Turkey is surprisingly modern (middle-aged and younger women don't wear veils; all children attend school), the Ellises showed boldness as they witnessed openly in a non-Christian country. In a similar way, when the Hebrew children faced a fiery furnace, they dared to tell the king they didn't fear death. They said, "If we are thrown into the blazing furnace, the God we serve is able to save us from it and he will rescue us from your hand" (Daniel 3:16–17). And God did save them, while their captors burned at the open door to the furnace (Daniel 3:22).

4. **You have great contentment in God.** I never saw the Ellises afraid, before, during, or after their trip. Even at their age, they had the assurance that God would take care of their health, allowing them opportunities to witness and return home safely.

M & M: Ministry and Missions Moment

One verse that can be used by nearly everyone is Philippians 4:11: "I have learned, in whatsoever state I am, therewith to be content" (KJV). This verse will prevent a nervous breakdown or a lifetime of worry. If you give this verse to someone else, you have blessed her or him with the idea of accepting life as it is. This week, design a card with this verse, and give it to someone, as God leads.

—— Study 18 ——

Two-by-Two Bible Studies
(Participant feedback from my three books.)

Most of your stress will be caused by not living as you know you should live. In other words, if you know Scriptures that should be directing your life, yet you're not following the Word in your workaday life, you will experience great stress. Any peace you experience will be the result of finding your place in God's plan and following that plan.

Practice What You Preach

The Old and New Testaments warn us against learning God's Word and not following its precepts in a daily practical way: "My people come to you, as they usually do, and sit before you to listen to your words, but they do not put them into practice" (Ezekiel 33:31). Jesus Himself identified those that didn't practice what they preached. He says, of the scribes and Pharisees: "Do not do what they do, for they do not practice what they preach" (Matthew 23:3).

Practice Hearing and Caring

Jesus said, "My mother and brothers are those who hear God's word and put it into practice" (Luke 8:21). Notice his family did two things: (1) hear the word, and (2) put it into practice.

Which activities in your life ensure that you hear the Word? Name them.

_____

_____

Which activities ensure that you put it into practice? Name them.

_____

_____

The Apostle Paul often instructed new Christians to practice hospitality and caring for others. You can practice hospitality by opening your home to someone. Teach her how to can tomatoes, quilt, or other things—whatever you like to do! Share your passion with her. Find common ground, so that through your friendship she will see Christ in you.

Paul said to Timothy, "If a widow has children or grandchildren, these should . . . put their religion into practice by caring for their own family" (1 Timothy 5:4), instead of putting a burden on the church to care for the widow. Scriptures and religious laws should be translated into action. When you do the right thing, word and deed walk hand in hand.

Follow Godly Examples

Paul said, "Whatever you have learned or received [realized] or heard from me, or seen in me—put into practice" (Philippians 4:9).

How would you define the difference between _learned_ and _realized_?

_____

_____

Explain "seen in me."

_____

_____

How have others seen Christ in you?

_____

_____

Increasing Fruit of the Spirit

Some Christians have unrealistic notions about spiritual maturity. They think it's an accomplishment. For example, when the Bible speaks of *fruit*, they take pride in the people they've "won" to the Lord, as if they're in a contest to see how many people they can win—as a notch on their belts. They may count the numbers of people who've become Christians because of their witnessing—and even keep an active, running list. Though we'd never admit it, we Christians are often proud of our salaries, education, community club memberships, or fame as Christian leaders.

Fruits emanate from your inner spirit. Someone said of a godly woman, "When she enters the room, she brings an aura, and it stays after she leaves." Have you ever known someone like that? You could almost feel the Holy Spirit as she spoke, served, and prayed.

"Shelly," an Ohio woman, came up to me and said, "I want to share the hurts I've experienced with other women. I've walked neck deep in troubled waters, and I don't know how to share all the wise words of Scripture, but I do want to share my home, share *myself*, with others."

Share Who You Are

Your person becomes evident as you become transparent. One mark of a maturing Christian is they become transparent when around others. They are willing to be vulnerable so others can succeed in life and in their Christian walk. Your in-walking can flow into the life of another's in-walking. As Paul says, you can help someone else be "nourished up in the words of faith" (1 Timothy 4:6 KJV).

Women as Hurt Magnets

Another woman came up and interrupted Shelly at the conference. "Where did you go?" she asked. "I need you to help me decide which things I need off this book table. I want to learn how to climb out of the hole I'm in. Help me make some wise choices."

Shelly teased her: "This woman has no patience yet, but she's on the right path to growing up in the Lord.

"I'm walking in the Spirit," said the second woman.

"And I'm a hurt magnet!" said Shelly. "Hurting women are drawn to me. Sometimes I think I have 'Tell me your troubles' written on my forehead." They laughed, nodding.

"She has the gift of mercy," The second woman said. "People sense her tender spirit and know she's sensitive to their needs."

Have you ever been a hurt magnet? Explain.

_____

_____

What kinds of personal experiences do you share to encourage women who are hurting?

_____

_____

_____

If appropriate, share your past experience with your study partner or a friend.

Bearing the Friendship Fruits

Jesus said, "By their fruit you will recognize them. . . . Every good tree bears good fruit" (Matthew 7:16–17); but He was not referring to new Christians others have witnessed to, or any other human accomplishments in religious service. His word identifies a Christian's fruit as unique traits of godly character: "The fruit of the Spirit is love, joy, peace, patience, kindness, goodness, faithfulness, gentleness (or mercy), and self-control" (Galatians 5:22–23a). He adds, "Against such things there is no law" (Galatians 5:23b). In other words, *Spiritual maturity grows these traits as by-products, the fruit from the tree of a fruitful, mature (or ripe) Christian. They can't be measured by the law, or a checklist of Scripture verses that will add up to 100 percent when all items are checked off.*

However, other people sense your spirit. If you interact with them, they'll know you're a Christian. There's something about you that attracts them, because you radiate the in-living Christ. Forming Christian friendships is one way you can introduce them to Scripture verses to draw them closer to Christ.

Two-by-Two Fellowships

Two by two, share yourself with another woman. She may be a niece who is not walking in the Spirit. Perhaps she's a friend God has shown you who needs more spiritual maturity. Share your spiritual fruits with her by being her friend and mentor, telling her what you know about His ways. Ask God first, "Show me your ways, O Lord" (Psalm 25:4). Then show her His ways. Teach her God's pathway and guide her in His truth.

Shelly and her friend decided to study my book *Friendships of Faith* together. As they studied the basics of God's Word in Hebrews, Shelly, the more mature woman, shared what she had learned through the years about Jesus. After she met the new Christian woman on Saturday mornings at a coffee shop, they shared what they'd learned in daily studies that week. Later they had lunch at Shelly's home. (Since her husband was Chinese, she taught Chinese cooking.) Over the years they bonded, as Shelly grew in her ability to share all of herself, the in-living Christ, and the living Word.

M & M: *Ministry and Missions Moment*

As you travel the road to a deeper spiritual maturity, you'll have your Savior beside you, with His love ever before you, His goodness and mercy following you all the days of your life, as He encourages you along the way. "Show me your ways, O Lord, teach me your paths; guide me in your truth and teach me, for you are God my Savior, and my hope is in you all day long" (Psalm 25:4–5). This week, begin a two-by-two Bible study, if God opens the door.

Study 19

Group Bible Studies

I was walking through my bedroom when the phone rang. "Hello," said a voice on the other end, "I just had to tell you about what's happened to our church." She explained that she was a women's leader in a large church with a series of fall Bible studies. As usual, different women's groups studied various Bible study books. She explained that most people—rather than study a topic—wanted to study a book of the Bible to get a coherent continuum of God's thought in His Word. Three of her groups had chosen *Friend to Friend: Enriching Friendships through a Shared Study of Philippians* but they were hardly aware of what others were studying.

Meanwhile, the church had been experiencing problems. One of the Bible study attendees was the daughter of the chairman of the deacons in their church. She and her father disagreed on several church issues. As the women chose sides on these issues, not only was the church splitting right down the middle, but also this daughter, Amie,* was splitting her family in half. Her mother and father chose one side, and she and her husband chose the other. The women in several Bible studies also had friction as each expressed her opinion of the church issues. Amie came often to Janelle, the leader who called me, complaining about women in the church that annoyed her. They celebrated the fellowship in her small Monday Bible study group, just beginning, which gave her a chance to vent the frustration she felt over the volatile outside situation in the church. Besides listening to Amie often, Janelle also had frequent visits from Melody, who also complained about someone in the church who always irritated her.

*Names in this story have been changed.

Have you ever known women at church who annoyed you? Explain.

_____

_____

Read Philippians 4:2–5. Write words God gives about Euodia and Syntyche that may apply to the women in your church.

_____

_____

_____

Have volatile outside situations in your church ever affected your small group of women in a missions or Bible study group? Explain.

_____

_____

_____

How could a small Bible study group bring unity in the whole church?

_____

_____

_____

Melody had just joined a Thursday group for the ten-week *Friend-to-Friend* course, to find new friends. Amie's mother joined Melody and the rest of the group, who agreed with Melody's position about the church issues. Janelle was happy about her women's discipleship program, and prayed that the many small groups would bond within. She celebrated that the only two complaints seemed related to others in the church and were beyond her power to quell.

Then a strange thing happened. Amie had finished studying Philippians 1:1 "From Paul and Timothy, servants of Christ Jesus," and rushed to tell Janelle how it had transformed her heart. With book in hand, she explained to Janelle that as she had learned about the principle of "under-ing" in a section called "We are never greater than our Master," she had memorized: "Our sinful nature is selfish and greedy. Staying under the authority of Jesus is counter to our natural instincts. Yet we read of spiritual giants like Paul . . . who have managed to stay focused on Him" (p. 9). Amie told Janelle, "I saw I was selfish and greedy, and I'd made the group agree with me. I was definitely not under the authority of Jesus in my life. I was under my own authority—and that of anyone who would agree with me, like these women in our group. I read in the section titled 'Because Daddy Said So' these words: 'Right is right and wrong is wrong, and you know the difference. . . . As a child of God you can choose to submit to God's rule' (p. 9). I realized I needed to submit to God's rule over my life, beginning with 'honor your father and mother.'"

Amie told Janelle, "This 'under-ing' really works. Once you get under the authority of Jesus, you can follow other authority. Today I talked to my father and asked his forgiveness. I've just come from my Bible study group and told them I was wrong. I begged them to go to other women in the church, and let's put this church back together."

Janelle said, "One of the most amazing things is that Amie was the young woman Melody hated, and Melody was the one

Amie hated, and I didn't have a clue. But God did, and the words in *Friend to Friend* put our church back together. They are now best friends, serving together under Christ's authority. We've had revival! Thank you for writing these words."

After we hung up, I thought back to the days when I was writing *Friend to Friend*. I had prayed, "God, you know I don't have the wisdom to write a Bible study. I just know how much I love Philippians and how it's changed my life. Just let your Holy Word change others as it has me."

I was dumbfounded as I recognized the power of Almighty God to heal a splintering, hurting church. I was thankful to Him and grateful to Janelle for calling me to let me know the mysterious way God had moved in her church. Two strong-willed women had found a way to change their church through a Bible study group. The group dynamics had exploded—as they always do, for good or for bad. With God in authority, this church lost its friction and united to serve Him in their community.

I've received other emails, letters, and phone calls from other women I didn't know who've studied *Friendships of Faith: A Shared Study of Hebrews and Friendships of Purpose: A Shared Study of Ephesians*. There's something about a small group dynamic that multiplies as the bond of unity in Christ solidifies. God can move out as you join your friends in a small group of friends and study God's Word together.

In small groups you will find the perfect *process* for centering on the pure Word of God and analyzing the indisputable truth. A discipleship group whose members sacrifice to meet weekly is encouraged to share in the Word, which leads to *light*. The light leads to *life*; new life leads to the *ability to see Christ*, and that sight leads to loving Christ, which leads to serving *Him as Lord*. A. W. Tozer says, "God's word is not opinion; it is truth"—but it shows up in the opinions you share in small groups as you dive into the Word.

Jesus: The Word of Authority

When Jesus finished the Sermon on the Mount, He ended with these words: "Not everyone who says to me, 'Lord, Lord,' will enter the kingdom of heaven, but only he who does the will of my Father who is in heaven" (Matthew 7:21). Then He told the story of the wise and foolish builders: "Everyone who hears these words of mine and puts them into practice is like a wise man who built his house on the rock" (Matthew 7:24). God's words are most powerful when maturing Christians put them into practice, just as the homeowner is wise when she or builds her house on the Solid Rock.

As we submit to the authority of God's Word, and anchor our souls on the Rock of the Scriptures, the word of truth liberates us from our carnal hang-ups and allows us to minister in His name.

Read John 8:32. Explain the meaning of this verse.

_____

_____

_____

_____

Have you experienced a truth in a small group Bible study that you'd never known before? Give an example.

_____

_____

_____

_____

_____

How has God spoken to you through a Scripture study that led you to a passion for a certain ministry? Explain.

_____

_____

_____

_____

_____

Don't Be Afraid of Tears

Watchman Nee says, "The Bible was written in tears; to tears it will yield its best treasure." All of us are different; some of us are emotional, some aren't. Be sensitive to the leading of the Holy Spirit as you share in a small group Bible study. As God speaks to individuals in the group, be ready to accept displays of emotion as the Bible comes alive. Also, if you're the leader, be ready to bring everyone back to the topic of the Scripture at the appropriate time.

God says, "The word of God is living and active. Sharper than any double-edged sword, it penetrates even to dividing soul and spirit. . . it judges the thoughts and attitudes of the heart" (Hebrews 4:12). Since God's truth sets us free, there's nothing more exhilarating than the freedom in a heart that's been imprisoned by fear and bondage. What a liberation from those hindrances that entangle and bind us (Hebrews 12:1)!

Growing Out of Group Study

Paul tells Timothy, "All Scripture is God-breathed and is useful for teaching, rebuking, correcting, and training in righteousness, so that the man (or woman) of God may be thoroughly equipped for every good work" (2 Timothy 3:16–17).

Be assured that if you allow Him, God will speak through His Scriptures as they teach, rebuke, correct, and train your group with passion for a ministry He's planned for you. "We are God's workmanship, created in Christ Jesus to do good works, which God prepared in advance for us to do" (Ephesians 2:10).

Which Work to Choose

You have a variety of works to do as God fills you with His passion for certain ministries. If you're interested in mission service, you may want to write to Volunteer Connection, P. O. Box 830010, Birmingham, AL 35283-0010 (or call 1-800-968-7301). Following Bible study, your group can go overseas or in the US to a variety of sites to witness and minister to people in need. If you want to teach conversational English to internationals visiting in your area, you may want to look for information at the North American Mission Board Web site (www.namb.net) or call 770-410-6000. If you'd like to mentor others in a lunch bunch, look for information at the Beautiful Hat Society Web site (www.thebeautifulhatsociety.com). This group meets for a short mentoring Bible study during lunchtime at a favorite restaurant.

Most Important Words of God

The most important work you can do as "His workmanship" (created as His precious servant) is to lead others to salvation. Here are Scriptures you might use in a group evangelism ministry, including a ministry of Scripture distribution.

1. All have sinned (done wrong things that hurt God, others, or ourselves). *All* includes you and me. "All have sinned and fall short of the glory of God" (Romans 3:23).
2. The penalty for sin is death. Therefore, since we have sinned, we deserve death. God is just. Since He rules with justice, He must punish sin. "The wages of sin is death" (Romans 6:23).

3. While God is just, He also is love. Because He loves us so much, He gave His only Son to die for us, taking our punishment. "But God demonstrates his own love for us in this: While we were still sinners, Christ died for us" (Romans 5:8).

4. If you confess Jesus is the Lord of your life, you will be saved from punishment and go to heaven, in His presence. "If you confess with your mouth 'Jesus is Lord,' and believe in your heart that God raised him from the dead, you will be saved" (Romans 10:9).

M & M: Ministry and Missions Moment

Watchman Nee also says, "God has nothing to say to the frivolous man." As a Christian, you have responsibilities as God's servant. Sometimes troubled times wake us up to our responsibilities and cause us to turn to God. Don't waste any time. Get real. Get serious about sharing Christ through Bible studies. Do it this week.

Study 20

Personal Bible Studies

Several times I've had a curious, special revelation from God through the Scriptures. One period of time I especially remember that God without a doubt spoke to me from His Word.

Working for the California Southern Baptist Convention in Fresno, I went to a conference in Alabama, where I met a man from a northeastern state who had attended a family funeral. His words took me aback when he offered me a job.

Years before, I had promised God I'd follow Him anywhere, and I had followed Him far beyond my imagination, first to Birmingham, and then to Fresno; but this job offer seemed to come out of nowhere. I believe that every incident in a Christian life has significance, either to bless us or teach us. Therefore, I began to pray and study God's Word to find out what He was up to. I asked Him to block this job offer if it were not His will and to show me clearly if it were. Even though it was way out of my comfort zone to move to the northeastern United States, I promised Him I would go if it were His will. Then I waited.

As I pored over the Scriptures with an intensity I hadn't experienced in months, I read these words in the Old Testament: "For I will take you out of the nations. . . ." [California was certainly a land of many nations . . . I thought of the daily planeloads of internationals who came into Fresno]. "I will gather you from all the countries and bring you back into *your own land*" (Ezekiel 36:24).

These words startled me. Where is my own land? Back east? In my hometown of Clinton, South Carolina?

"Lord, are you about to move me out?" No response.

The next day, reading the following Scripture passage revealed these words: "You will live in the land I gave your forefathers" (Ezekiel 36:28).

On the following day, I read: "I will put my spirit in you . . . and I will settle you in your own land. . . and *I have done it*, declares the Lord" (Ezekiel 37:14). I paused. "Oh, my. He's about to move me out!" I thought, as I prayed seriously about new directions.

One night I prayed, "Lord, this isn't my plan. I don't want to leave California. I love the weather! I love my supervisor. Jack loves it here; he has a good job. Moving is just not in our plan." I turned to that day's reading in my devotional book: "In him we were also chosen, having been predestined according to THE PLAN OF HIM who works out everything in conformity WITH THE PURPOSE OF HIS WILL" (Ephesians 1:11). My capitalized words were those that jumped off the page of my Bible. I focused on *His plan. His purpose. His will.*

I prayed again, "Lord, you've placed a burden on me. I can't take time to think of this right now. A move . . . I don't know." Then I read further in Ephesians: "I keep asking that the God of our Lord Jesus Christ, the glorious Father, may give you the Spirit of wisdom and revelation, so that you may know him better. I pray that the eyes of your heart will be enlightened" (Ephesians 1:17–18).

I could hardly believe the Scripture, which was a conversation-style talk with God.

"Lord, when are you going to enlighten me? *How* are you going to enlighten me? I need answers."

I read from another devotional Scripture: "The wise heart will know the proper time and procedure" (Ecclesiastes 8:5).

I went for a job interview and was approved by a nominating

committee and then a large board as a worker in the new area. The state's executive director said, "Everything's cleared. I hope you'll give us a yes answer in the morning."

I slept little that night. My son, Jack, who'd gone with me, had spent the day kayaking and hiking with young men on the staff. He loved the area, but before bed that night, we both prayed for definite directions from God. That night, I got down on my knees and prayed desperately. "O God, I don't like to waste money. These good people have paid for Jack and me to come here to see if it's Your will at work. All is set. Everything's approved. We only lack one thing. I have to know your will by in the morning. I want to know now!"

No response. I spent hours that night praying and reading Scripture.

Finally, I said, "Lord, I'm going to be embarrassed in the morning when they ask for my answer. I'm going to look stupid when I have no answer for them. I'm willing to do Your will. What do you want me to say?"

No response.

Then I read Isaiah 49:8, hearing these words in a stern, almost-audible voice: "In the time of MY favor I will answer you."

"Oh . . . OK, Lord. Forgive me for being so bigheaded. I'm sorry. It's not my embarrassment I ought to be thinking about. It's about pleasing You." Like Isaiah when he saw God high and lifted up in the tabernacle (Isaiah 6:1-5), I felt awkward in the presence of the living God, a woman with unclean lips.

"Uh, I'm going to hush now and go to sleep." And I did.

I didn't have an answer the next day, and the state leaders understood. I stopped fretting, waiting about a week, and finally told them that—hearing nothing from God—I'd better not move from where I was.

A few weeks later I received a job offer in which God did move me from the "land of many nations" back to the South, where I could be closer to my mother for the two years before she died. It was, without a doubt, the place where God wanted me.

Purity Growing out of God's Word

The job-offer trip taught me tremendous truths about God. First, I was a sinful mortal who needed more spiritual maturity. Second, my insistence on an immediate answer to satisfy human rules of conduct was totally out of line. My demanding was probably offensive to the Almighty. Third, I needed to be patient, be still—really still—and get to know God better. He says, "Be still, and know that I am God" (Psalm 46:10). Since that week, I have spent more time in personal Bible study.

God does not want you to come to Him on your knees, desperately seeking His will only when you are in crisis: when a decision needs to be made hurriedly, when your back is against the wall. He wants you to come to Him *kneeling in your heart*, spiritually humble; ready to set aside all you have to do today just to talk to Him. He wants your complete attention. And He wants your obedience to Scripture.

Read Isaiah 42:19–20. Explain what this passage tells you about your disciplined study of God's Word.

_____

_____

_____

_____

_____

_____

How can you become a better reader? List things to do in Bible study.

_____

_____

_____

_____

How can you become a better listener? List things to do as you listen to His voice while studying.

_____

_____

_____

_____

_____

_____

_____

All of us stand in need of personal purity, which grows out of God's Word. Your personal purity grows as you make the following requests, like the psalmist.

Five Requests for Personal Purity

"Show me your ways, O Lord, teach me your paths; guide me in your truth and teach me, for you are God my Savior, and my hope is in you all day long" (Psalm 25:4–5).

1. Show me Your ways.
2. Teach me Your paths.
3. Guide me in Your truth.
4. Help me acknowledge You as Savior.
5. Give me hope in You all day long.

Make a list of books of the Bible or certain passages that in your opinion are "must reads" for people looking for a daily devotion, for personal purity before God.

_____

_____

_____

_____

_____

_____

Share your list with others who are following the discipline of a daily devotion.

See also at the end of this book the list of recommended books to read as a companion for the Bible, for a walk toward personal purity.

The Word Blocked by Impurity

Spiritual power cannot pass through a personality where impurity and resentment live. If you expect to refine your heart in personal purity, consider any signs of anger or resentment. Recall things you'd consider impure in your life. Ask God for forgiveness and make things right with others as well as with Him. He says, "If you hold anything against anyone, forgive him" (Mark 11:25). Take a hard look at your heart and estimate in which areas you need forgiveness and improvement in obedience and habits.

Pray, using this verse: "Search me, O God, and know my heart; test me and know my anxious thoughts. See if there is any offensive way in me, and lead me in the way everlasting" (Psalm 139:23).

The Word Blocked by the World

God also says, "The cares of this world . . . choke the word" (Matthew 13:22 NKJV). The NIV says: "the worries of this life and the deceitfulness of wealth choke it." Consider lifestyle factors that may corrupt your heart so it can't respond to God's Word. Ask God to take away any obsessions with possessions, impurity, anger, resentment, and/or any dissatisfaction about relationships you may have. Pray this Scripture verse: "May integrity and uprightness protect me, because my hope is in you" (Psalm 25:21). Ask God to open your heart in new ways to accept the Holy Spirit as you read His Word. Pray specifically for a pure heart. (For more information on a pure heart, read *Deeper Still: A Woman's Study to a Closer Walk with God*, Study 3 and Study 26.)

Pure and Personal, not Puritanical and Prudish

Personal purity begins when you accept Christ as Savior. It doesn't derive from perfection of God's law, but from your completion in Christ, being permeated with His Word. If there's any possibility you've never accepted Christ into your heart, stop now, follow the plan of salvation in Study 19, and share your decision with your pastor or a Bible study partner. Be sure you have assurance of salvation before you move further to develop a pure heart.

When God's Word says, "Be perfect . . . as your heavenly Father is perfect" (Matthew 5:48) and "You shall be holy for I your God am holy" (Leviticus 19:2), scholars sometimes translate the word *perfect, teleos, as "complete"*: "Be complete as your father is complete" He wants to complete you through Jesus Christ your Lord. He doesn't require you to have a stiff, sour, puritanical or prudish attitude. He wants you to have a pure heart, cleansed by Christ's blood.

One part of your daily devotion training is a desire for godliness. The heart-refining process, or sanctification, has eternal consequences. All purity of heart has an eternal quality that is significant for the immediate and distant future. Paul said, "Train yourself to be godly. For physical training is of some value, but godliness has value for all things, holding promise for both the present life and the life to come" (1 Timothy 4:7–8).

M & M: Ministry and Missions Moment

How do you know if you have personal purity? You often don't know. Here are the signs you may recognize in yourself: You're eager to set aside time for Bible study. You can't wait to get to church events to hear the Word of God preached. You love your Bible. You have absorbed many verses and can quote them in situations where they apply to life. You have inner peace when all the world is chaotic around you.

Jesus says, "I have come that they may have life, and . . . have it more abundantly" (John 10:10 NKJV). May you have abundant life as you engage in personal Bible study this week.

Unit 5

———————— • ————————

KEEPING YOUR
EYES ON JESUS

Whether you are a novice in prayer or an experienced prayer warrior, you recognize that prayer is a powerful force in the world, and it's often misunderstood. During the tough times of life, you are too self-focused—distracted by misery—to see the effects of prayer. Then you begin to see prayer as healing for the body, soul, and spirit. You deal a death blow to pride and ego, and as you do, you soar in prayer. As you grow in Him, you take a leadership of one among those near you. Look around you. You'll find people in need of your assurance as you pray for them. Now's the time to learn a new meaning—a new definition—for *intercession*.

Prayer is not an instant solution. Nor is it an exercise in begging. It's a supernatural spot in time in which your spirit mingles with the Spirit of Almighty God and the Holy Comforter. Yes, prayer changes the world, but the most important thing it changes is *you*.

. . . .

O Lord, I pray that every day
You'll help me dare to do what's right.
I pause to pray for times I live
In fear and darkness and poor sight.
    And help me bend my knees in prayer
    And see your loving face of light.

                     —*ee*

. . . .

—— Study 21 ——

Prayer as Healing

Sharon Fields McCormick (whom I mentioned in Study 1) tells this story: one morning as a young graduate student, she became ill with a terrible pain in her right side. Knowing she had no medical insurance, she decided to sweat it out at home, where she lay doubled up all day. Unable to bear the excruciating pain any longer, she went to a walk-in clinic. The doctor diagnosed appendicitis and told her to go to a hospital for surgery. Instead, giving the clinic her last funds, Sharon started home. Her boyfriend asked her to let his mother pray for her. Their denomination believed in faith healing, he said; but Sharon hesitated, since her own Baptist denomination didn't emphasize faith healing. The boyfriend's mother prayed for Sharon anyway. Nothing happened. Sharon smiled through her pain and lay down. She had learned about faith and prayer, so she began to pray: "I have faith, O God, that you will heal me eventually," thinking that after the surgery she would be fine.

Suddenly she felt a wave of warmth wash over her from head to toe. Hardly able to believe it, she felt no pain. She stood up straight for the first time that day. She was healed!

Sharon has often pondered the situation. God allowed her to meet a boyfriend who introduced her to his mother, who believed in faith healing. Sharon then acted in faith, asking God to heal her. When the doctor later called, confirming her appendicitis, to be sure she made it to the hospital, she told him how God had healed her! He was in charge of all circumstances in Sharon's life.

Besides His Holy Word, God speaks to humankind in several ways: revelation through the process of prayer; visions; and dreams. These experiences bring about physical, emotional, mental, and spiritual healing. Healing is a process in which God and humans cooperate.

It is common knowledge that sick people whose Christian friends pray for them heal faster and more completely. Even when patients in hospitals don't know people are praying for them, blind studies prove they have a better percentage of recovery. Furthermore, scientific research shows people of faith can lower their blood pressure through prayer. Physically and scientifically, prayer heals.

However, there is much more to the mystical process of prayer than the physical side or the repetition of words, such as the Lord's Prayer, or the Prayer of St. Francis of Assisi. God works a supernatural miracle each time a Christian prays. Your life may be the answer to someone's prayer prayed thousands of years ago. God's Spirit works in mysterious ways to fulfill His people's requests.

God says: "I will pour out my Spirit on all people. Your sons and daughters will prophesy, your old men will dream dreams, your young men will see visions" (Joel 2:28). In tough times like today, when open evangelism isn't allowed in many countries, God finds ways to speak to His people. The twenty-first century is a time of dreaming dreams, especially in Third World countries, where the gospel is forbidden.

Missionaries and other Christians around the world frequently tell stories about nonbelievers having dreams or visions. Years ago, when missionaries in Kenya reached a previously unreached village, an older woman welcomed them, saying, "All my life I've waited for you to come. I once had a dream that Christians would come. I didn't know who Christians were, but a man named Jesus in my dream told me not to worship until you came to tell me more about Him."

Ask About the Name

More recently a young Asian man, trained from age four to be a Buddhist monk, served as a beggar, sitting by the side of a busy road. One day he was hit by a car, hurting his leg so badly doctors planned to amputate the next day. He slept restlessly in the hospital and had a dream: someone in his dream looked at his leg and said, "Your leg will be fine."

He asked, "What's your name?"

"Jesus."

The next day the monk refused to have his leg amputated. It miraculously healed in a few days. Each day he looked for someone named Jesus, to thank Him. One day a traveling evangelist came by and asked, "Do you know the living God?"

The monk shook his head sadly.

The evangelist said, "He sent His Son to earth for you. His Son's name is Jesus."

The monk jumped up. "Yes, I know Him! He healed me. Tell me how to know Him better." He became a Christian that day, left his begging place, and spent the rest of his life telling others about the Lord of his dream.

Prayers of Faith: Pray in Jesus's Name

The Lord of the beggar's dream is the Lord of all prayers. God's Word teaches you to pray in Jesus's name. Be assured He's the Lord of the realm of prayer. You pray in Jesus's name because He's your mediator, connection to the Godhead, and access to heaven. Jesus said, "I will do whatever you ask *in my name*" (John 14:13).

Read Acts 3:1–10 and summarize how divine power was displayed in Jesus's name.

_____

_____

_____

_____

The disciples often prayed in Jesus's name. One afternoon at 3:00, their traditional prayer time, Peter and John entered the temple in Jerusalem by the Beautiful Gate, where a lame man asked for money. As Peter said, "Silver or gold I do not have, but what I have I give you. *In the name of Jesus Christ of Nazareth*, walk" (Acts 3:6), He joined God in a miracle of healing! When the astonished Jews followed Peter and John to a colonnade, Peter explained: "By faith *in the name of Jesus*, this man . . . was made strong. It is Jesus's name and the faith that comes through him that has given this complete healing to him" (Acts 3:16).

Persistent Prayers: Pray from Your Heart

Since your prayers are communications with God, the mode of prayer will reflect your heart. When your heart is happy, your prayers include thanksgiving and praise. During troubled times, your prayers primarily include petitions and pleas as you lay your needs before Him. Sometimes people have the unfounded idea that they don't need to "bother" God with their aches and pains. Yet Matthew 7:7–11 is translated: "Keep on asking; keep on seeking; keep on knocking." The imperfect Greek tense has the sense of continuing action. God might be saying, "Go ahead; bother me. Keep on bothering me. I love it when we talk." Just as good parents wait for a child to ask the right questions, your heavenly Father may be whispering, "Come on, ask me. I've already made preparations to bless you, dear child; I've been waiting for you to ask."

Bonding Prayers: Pray with Intercession

As needs arise, your heart will reach out in intercessory prayers for others. When my son-in-law worked for an unscrupulous supervisor, my daughter called to explain the situation. "Mom," she said. "Please pray for Tim. He's in a tight place at work. He doesn't want to do anything unethical. He's applied for a job with another company. Please ask God to open the new job opportunity, if it's God's will. We need prayer power now."

I prayed for Tim's job fervently and hourly, over the next few days.

In four days, Tim called. "You can get off your knees now," he said.

"What?"

"I got the new job," he said.

"Oh, praise the Lord! My prayers were answered!"

"Thank you," said Tim. From then on, we had a special mother-in-law/son-in-law bond. Prayer joins hearts in an intercessory prayer focus. It's the strongest adhesive, strengthening family ties and Christian fellowship because the name of Jesus invokes a supernatural element of truth and power into the process.

Prayer is calling home every day. God loves to talk with you.

Supernatural Prayer: Pray with Expectancy

Prayer is a place where your spirit meets the Holy Spirit. Christians experience a spirit of excitement as they interact with Almighty God! His Spirit is sometimes called the "hound of heaven" because He vigorously seeks you. Prayer is a place where you learn from Him, and He molds you to His will, showing you God's unbelievable grace, which brings total healing. As you pray, you learn to see yourself as you really are—as all of us are—full of self. Sometimes you realize that even work for our church and community is selfishly motivated. Since the Holy Spirit is light personified (John 8:12), He reveals your sinful self as you open your communication with Him.

As you pray, God prepares you for more light. Every day, every year, you'll find more dark corners to give to Christ, to expose to the Holy Spirit's light.

Energizing Prayer: Pray with Power

God says, "Those who hope in the Lord will renew their strength. They will soar on wings like eagles; they will run and not grow weary, they will walk and not be faint" (Isaiah 40:31). The Hebrew word *renew* is translated "exchange." Prayer is the place where you exchange depression for happiness, evil for good, and hate for love.

Write what the following verses explain about God's power.

Philippians 3:12–14:

_____

_____

_____

_____

2 Corinthians 6:4–10:

_____

_____

_____

_____

Ephesians 6:10–20:

_____

_____

_____

_____

Pray for Spiritual Healing around the World

One way to lead others to pray is to share your intercessory prayers with them. As a creative prayer reminder, copy the following and place it in a small plastic bag, with an assortment of hard-shelled candy (M&M's, Reese's Pieces, etc.).

Like this candy has a hard shell and sweet center, people often have hard shells, not trusting strangers. Melting the shell reveals sweet, soft candy inside. Pray that missionaries will be able to get through the shell and reach unsaved people for Christ.

1. Brown represents people who live in darkness. Pray that Jesus's light will penetrate the darkness of disbelief and false religions.
2. Yellow represents light. Pray that missionaries can be channels for showing the light and love of Jesus. Pray that they'll be a light that challenges and dispels evil in the darkness.
3. Blue represents newness. Pray for new missionaries in new places. Ask God to help them overcome homesickness, adjusting to a new culture. Pray for new believers to grow in spiritual wisdom.
4. Red represents danger. (Red dye in candy was considered dangerous, but it's now declared safe.) Pray for those exiled from a dangerous country/facing persecution if they stay.

5. Green represents fertility. Pray for areas not yet ripe for harvest, that seeds will be planted, take root, and grow.
6. Orange represents fruit. Pray that missionaries will reap a harvest of souls, and that people will not hesitate but promptly accept the truth.

Patient Prayers: Pray with Calm Trust

The Complete Idiot's Guide to Prayer says prayer teaches us humility and patience. Just as a patient in the hospital has to be patient, you must be patient in prayer. This year I've seen three people undergo knee surgery. Usually they experience pain at first, but in a few days, with patience they recover and feel much better physically, mentally, and spiritually. No matter what the answer is, pray with calm trust. Like a child who begs for candy but needs vegetables, God answers your prayers with the best for you.

Deep Calls to Deep

The psalmist says to God, "Deep calls to deep in the roar of your waterfalls; all your waves and breakers have swept over me. By day the Lord directs his love, at night his song is with me—a prayer to the God of my life" (Psalm 42:7–8). If you are willing to go deeper into God's Spirit, in the deep place where you allow your spirit to mingle with His, God will heal you physically, mentally, emotionally, and spiritually. May you find health in every area of your life through the Spirit who calls you to the depths.

M & M: Ministry and Missions Moment

Deep calls to deep. Is God calling you deeper now? If you want to know what it's like deep in the heart of God, pray. If you're troubled and experiencing tough times, prayer is the place where God sets everything right. Spend more time in personal prayer this week.

Study 22

Leadership in Prayer

At the battle of Fredericksburg, a South Carolina soldier, Richard Kirkland, gave a drink of water to those who were dying, whether in blue or gray uniforms. He said, "A man that brave deserves it." Others called Kirkland the "angel of Mary's Heights," the small hill where he had courage to step out of character as a vicious soldier and love all humanity. Afterward, soldiers revered Mary's Heights; one said, "Peace settles when we kneel here to pray." Kirkland took a stand in a gesture of peace and others followed his example. Many great leaders have also made prayer their watermark. George Washington knelt in the snow at Valley Forge, and people often saw Abraham Lincoln in his office window praying before he made big decisions. We take heart when we know our leaders pray.

Check the following statements that most likely describe you.

____ I have never prayed in public.

____ I am afraid to pray when others are listening.

____ I believe in God and in prayer, but admit I don't spend time praying.

____ I pray constantly.

____ I pray and read my Bible a certain time every day.

___ I am a prayer warrior, praying in intercession for the sick, lost, and endangered.

___ I am thrilled when I hear the prayers of others.

___ I wish my family prayed more.

___ I wish I led others more frequently in prayer.

___ I've taught many people to pray.

___ I'm a leader in a prayer group.

Leadership of One

In 1 Samuel 17:38–39, we read about the time Israel's King Saul talked with David, still a shepherd boy, as he was about to face the giant Goliath. "Then Saul dressed David in his own tunic. He put a coat of armor on him and a bronze helmet on his head. David fastened on his sword over the tunic and tried walking around, because he was not used to them. 'I cannot go in these,' he said to Saul, 'because I am not used to them.' So he took them off."

Perhaps you're a prayer warrior, but your children have disappointed you. Others in your family or circle of friends may have not taken up the mantle, as Elisha did after the famous prophet Elijah was taken up to heaven (2 Kings 2:9–15). You yearn for them to lead in prayer as you've done.

On the other hand, you may feel awkward praying in public or leading anyone in any kind of prayer ministry. You don't fit your mother's "prayer uniform"—or that of some godly prayer warrior in your church. However, David, a young shepherd without any experience in leadership, stepped out in faith, becoming even greater than King Saul. David said, "The Lord who delivered me from the paw of the lion . . . will deliver me from the hand of this Philistine." Like David, you can become a prayer warrior. Like Saul, you can train others to become prayer warriors. Both David and

Elisha became greater than their leaders. Begin now praying that you can be a leadership of one to help other family members and young women you mentor to be giants of prayer.

Virginia Wilson, in *Lose the Halo, Keep the Wings*, said, "If you are known as a woman of prayer, you will also be known as a woman of power." Step out in power in a leadership of one; working with children, teens, or adults in your home, neighborhood, or church. Though, like David, they must fight the giants of life in their own way, you can teach them what you know about prayer.

Can you remember people who were your examples of pray-ers? List them here.

_____

_____

_____

Which of their characteristics do you wish you had?

_____

_____

Which characteristics have you passed to the next generation?

_____

_____

What traits do you have that would make you a good prayer teacher?

_____

_____

I'm Not Able

God says, "What I am commanding you today is not too difficult for you or beyond your reach" (Deuteronomy 30:11). Don't say leading others in prayer is too hard. God is able. He calls on the weak to prove His power. Remember, Noah drank too much; Abraham was too old; Jeremiah and Timothy were too young; Isaac was a day-dreamer; Jacob was a liar; Leah was ugly; Joseph was abused; Moses stuttered; Rahab was a prostitute; Isaiah preached naked; Jonah had a bad attitude; John the Baptist ate bugs; Martha worried about everything; Job went bankrupt, and Lazarus was dead! Yet each of these had a place in the Bible as a godly person redeemed by God.

Which Bible characters do you think were unlikely leaders?

_____

_____

What qualified them to be mentioned in the Bible?

_____

_____

Pick out one character above. Look up the name in a Bible concordance or on the Internet.

_____

_____

How did God bless this character?

_____

_____

What do you have in common with him/her?

_____

_____

Has God nudged you to choose a prayer partner with whom you'll pray for concerns? If not, why not? If so, what have you done about His nudging?

Write the names of people whom you might mentor in prayer:

At home: _____

_____

In my extended family:_____

_____

At work:_____

_____

At school:_____

_____

At church: _____

_____

In my community:_____

_____

God-Led Ways to Serve

God can lead you in a variety of prayer ministries. You may want to start a prayer chain. One person activates the chain by calling a leader with requests; then one by one, word goes by phone to activate the prayers. (See Study 25.)

You may organize several people with whom you pray weekly. I once prayed with a group of busy women every morning at 10:00, wherever we were. Participants might have been sewing, cooking, on coffee break at work, walking a dog, rocking a baby, or trimming shrubbery. We knew the others would join with us in prayer in all situations.

Prayerwalking is a great combination of exercise and prayer. Pray with your eyes open as you walk, stopping as God leads, to pray for a certain home, business, school, or yard. Praying for people you meet on a prayerwalk will change their lives as well as yours. You may prayerwalk alone, but most Christians pray and walk together as they engage in this ministry.

Designing and distributing prayer reminders is a needed ministry today. Gather small cards, scrapbooking materials, and lists of prayer requests you could print on the cards and distribute to prayer warriors. Another prayer ministry is visiting hospitals, nursing homes, shut-ins, or retirement centers, praying individually for each person. One rewarding ministry waits for you in halfway houses, women's/children's shelters, and soup kitchens. Most of these places welcome someone who cares.

Does your church have a prayer room? If not, think how you could furnish one, with a kneeling bench, pillows, easy chairs, and lists of prayer requests. Most prayer rooms have a small file box with prayer requests on cards, on which you sign your name and the date after you've prayed. You or someone else can help with updating the cards.

If your church has weekly churchwide prayer meetings, your ministry may be gleaning prayer requests from members and the community at large, printing them on one sheet, and distributing them before the meeting.

Cottage prayer meetings in homes all over town and all-night prayer vigils are appropriate for special times of renewal in your church.

If you like to read and have the gift of administration, you could be the "Office of Record" for prayer in your area. Keep prayer requests from religious magazines, daily newspaper headlines, and word of mouth. Keep them available for others who call your prayer line.

Believe in Prayer

Once when my husband headed to our farm to plow all day, he prayed that he would be able to witness that day. His prayer was answered in dramatic ways. A man on the wrong road drove by to ask for directions and heard about Jesus. A forestry expert stopped to ask the price of trees in a grove nearby and heard about Jesus. A hunter stepped out of the trees near our cornfield and stayed to receive Jesus as his Savior! (The gun unnerved my husband a bit, but he kept talking.) God provides miracles when you pray.

M & M: Ministry and Missions Moment

If you don't see a prayer ministry in sight, ask God to give you one. Right now, you can step out in a leadership of one, empowered *for* prayer, *by* prayer. Choose at least one idea from this study and use it this week. Pray that God will show you how to lead others as you give your prayer service to Him.

——— Study 23 ———

Praying for Others with Serious Problems

Five words symbolize a praying life: *taste, place, erase, lace,* and *grace.*

Taste the Cup of Suffering

First, you need to taste the cup of suffering. Every human being experiences hard times. Even Jesus asked God to take His suffering away. "My Father, if it is possible, may this cup be taken from me. Yet not as I will, but as you will" (Matthew 26:39). Yet, since you live in the world, pain is a part of your human mortality. Your hurts during troubled times can refine your heart and give you the depth of character to intercede for others. Every pray-er must experience the depths, but as a maturing Christian pray-er who reflects on these deeper things, you release your roots, reaching into your heart core, growing still deeper in God's love. Your pains, tests, and trials prepare your heart for intercessory prayer.

You've heard it said that prayer works because prayer is work. The serious pray-er is willing to do the work, not as a slave to a task of hard toil, but as co-worker with God. The prayer process is *joyous work for an audience of one,* for you pray to please *Him.*

Place Your Spirit in God's Place

Second, preparing for intercessory prayer requires your being in a certain place. No, this is not your breakfast table, your favorite chair, a chapel, or another special place where you pray. Neither is this *place* an act of setting aside things such as a Bible, prayer list, or prayer calendar arranged in your special prayer place—although those things are important. This *certain place* is a place of the heart. It is a Christian centering, moving your thoughts toward the depths of God's thoughts, your feelings toward the depths of His feelings. Begin as you would with an old friend, welcoming His Spirit into your heart. Praise Him for who He is, what He has done, and what He's doing now in our life. Spend a few moments joyously praising Him. Just sit and listen.

When other thoughts interfere, write those down quickly to handle later. Get them out of your spirit so you can enjoy only the Holy Spirit's presence. In her book, *Spiritual Life Development*, Mildred McMurray says, "Whenever a soul is on fire with love and compassion for others, it is the result of a conscious union of the person with God through prayer."

Erase Yourself

Placing your spirit in God's Spirit takes unselfishness. It's true that the all-day, every-moment praying of a constant Christian prayer warrior is effective: "The effectual fervent prayer of a righteous man availeth much" (James 5:16 KJV). However, for a deeper walk in the place of the Spirit's in-living, stop the day's chores, take time out, sit down, and listen to what God wants to say. When I was married, I kept busy scurrying around the house doing chores, never taking time to sit. Occasionally my husband would say, "Edna, slow down. Come over here; sit and talk with me." Those quiet moments without frantic activity saved my marriage. We needed down time together. Sometimes we're so absorbed in self and the tasks with which we stay busy to maintain self that we have no time for prayer. McMurray also said, "Real prayer begins by dealing a death blow to pride and egoism." I call this "erasing yourself." Praise

God, thanking Him for blessings. Confess your sin daily, and then listen before you bring God your petitions. Remember, before you pray, erase your agenda, and seek God's deep place.

Lace Your Character with Concern for Others

Most Christians who are serious about praying keep a running list of people for whom they pray. They also keep lists of agencies who can help give answers to prayer (for example Christian psychologists/psychiatrists who offer counseling to people with serious mental illnesses, or safe houses to offer refuge for abused people). They know the names of missionaries (Prayer Patterns in *Missions Mosaic* magazine is a good source of missionary names—visit www.womenonmission.com; *Mission Frontiers* also offers up-to-date information as prayer fodder—www.missionfrontier.org). They also know their prayers change circumstances on the other side of the world. They're ready to suggest needs for which you could pray, because they have a bond with all humanity, regardless of nationality, race, or culture.

If you're a maturing pray-er, you'll find yourself praying more often, for more extended periods each time. You'll also find you reach out physically to others, sincerely caring, after you have prayed for them spiritually. Your heart becomes more tender, and you possess more mercy in all sorts of situations.

Bonhoeffer once said something that changed my life: "Intercession is the most promising way to reach our neighbors; and corporate prayer offered in the name of Christ, the purest form of fellowship." If you're maturing your praying life, you're passionate about corporate as well as personal prayer. You eagerly await your weekly prayer group that prays for serious situations and breakthroughs of the gospel worldwide. You organize a prayer group meeting in your home. Your prayer life is vital, active, and vigorous. In short, life-giving concern for others laces your character.

Grace Your Life with Prayers of Peace

In *Following in His Train*, Ethlene Boone Cox said, "Prayer is an awesome realm. It creates peace out of chaos, love out of hate, activity out of lethargy." Without leaving your recliner chair, you can change the world. Because God is greater than you are, He explodes your puny grace into magnified grace.

List places in the world that need peace.

_____

_____

_____

Write your prayer for each of these places.

_____

_____

_____

_____

_____

_____

_____

_____

The world can become more peaceful as your spirit mingles with God's in prayer. As you find grace enough to interact with others, praying for them in sincere concern, God *does* create peace out of chaos, love out of hate, activity out of lethargy—in your heart and in the hearts of others as you relate to them. Paul says to fellow

Christians, "This service that you perform is not only supplying the needs of God's people but is also overflowing in many expressions of thanks to God" (2 Corinthians 9:12). When you minister to others, they thank God for your works in His name. Your prayers and ministry become a catalyst in others, turning them to prayers of thanksgiving. "Because of the service by which you have proved yourselves, men will praise God for the obedience that accompanies your confession of the gospel of Christ, and for your generosity in sharing with them and with everyone else. And in their prayers for you their hearts will go out to you, because of the surpassing grace God has given you. Thanks be to God for his indescribable gift!" (2 Corinthians 9:13-15).

Take time now to thank God for His ever-present grace.

Taste, Place, Erase, Lace, and Grace

Remember these words: *Taste* the cup of suffering as an exercise in obedience. God builds your character for prayer only after you've experienced some deep, tough times. As you accept God's discipline, you *place* your spirit in God's place, where His Spirit dwells. As you absorb His Spirit, *erase* yourself. Think "other." Get serious about serious problems among your friends, community, and world. *Lace* your character with concern for others. *Grace* your life with prayers of peace.

M & M: Ministry and Missions Moment

One final word on serious praying: Cox also said prayer could bring love out of hate and *activity out of lethargy*. Get going! This week, may you allow God to help you be alert, alive, and enthusiastic about prayer.

Study 24

Prayer Journals: Individuals and Groups

My former Bible study teacher kept extensive notes in journals. She could not bring herself to tell her own children what pain she suffered each day, but wrote her prayers to God "for release," she said, so the pain would pass. Soon she felt better and could be a sweet blessing for her children, not a nagging, sour widow who made her children feel guilty or sad about her life. She kept another journal in which she wrote more prayers to God, which included insights on how to pray and advice to her children about how to find the most joy in Christ in their day-to-day lives. She planned to leave this prayer journal to them as a legacy, hoping they'd read it, profiting from her mistakes and triumphs.

You may want to write a prayer journal, like many other Christians, for several reasons.

For Release

Writing is a release when you're troubled. Like the Bible study teacher, you may write your dreary thoughts to "get them out of your system." To keep from expressing your pain or hurt, you can write about them as you pray, and somehow God brings relief. Writing distracts the human spirit from its body-fascination with pain. Nothing beats the combination of writing and praying for lifting your spirits. During times of tension, the quiet withdrawal to a calm corner to write in your prayer journal gives release from anxiety. It's OK to have a place where you vent in a private way—just between you and Him.

Write a prayer you may have prayed as a release during a troubled time.

_____

_____

_____

_____

_____

For a Reality Check

If you record your prayers to God each day, you can look back and see where you've been. Reading words you wrote from your heart to His, you may see how you have progressed, or backslidden, as you chart spiritual development over the months.

For example, you may see yourself in your journal at an immature point. Looking back on several situations, you can see God gave you the sensible elements you needed for growth, rather than the foolish baubles you requested that would've made you spiritually emaciated. You may find other entries in your journal that prove the verses about the mustard seeds' bringing larger results years later than you ever imagined when you prayed the tiny prayers of weakling faith. Reviewing your journal entries provides a reality check for you to see yourself as you really are—and as you've grown spiritually as time has passed.

Recall how your prayers show your Christian maturation progress over the years.

Words from your childhood prayers:

_____

Words from later prayers:

_____

Words you pray today:

_____

_____

For Privacy

Some things you write in your private journal you'd never tell in public. Don and Judy Allison in Virginia tell a wonderful testimony of being in the right place at the right time, but it's one they don't tell. Judy wrote this down and later shared it with me.

One Saturday a stomach problem prevented Don from going on a motorcycle ride. Though he regretted he couldn't get too far from the house, he decided to spend the time on a useful pursuit: studying the Sunday School lesson he was teaching the next day. He'd just begun studying when he had an urge to visit the powder room. As he entered, he looked out the window and noticed Carol, a short, little neighbor, struggling to raise a ladder to the top of their two-story house. Looking closer, he realized her husband was stuck on the roof. Immediately Don went over to their house to raise the ladder. After he helped Carol's husband down, both of them expressed appreciation over and over. It would have been impossible for Carol to get him down without Don's assistance. "It's amazing," Don said to them without fully explaining "how God will get you from one place to another."

Immediately Don's stomach problem was gone. He was fine, but God had gotten him to a window to see a neighbor's need. They were thankful he had to stay home that day!

Whatever your private thoughts, you can write them to God in a journal and know they'll be safe there. If your thoughts are sinful, irritable, or off-color, writing them between you and God is acceptable. If you're tired, frustrated, or disrespectful, God understands. He knows your heart.

For Posterity

One of the greatest reasons for having a journal is to leave a legacy for your children (or friends' children, nieces, etc.). My cousin, Earl Martin, has written about his childhood and his extended family. His mother died before his children knew her, and he's now found a way to tell them how life was when she was young. He's given his children something he never had as a young man. His father never told him how life was when the father was a child. Now that both his parents are gone, Earl regrets he doesn't have them to ask about family history. In fact, Earl and I are planning to write the *Martin Family Memories*, or some similar title, which will include segments from Shirley, Jean, Phyllis, Lee, Robert, Lynn, and other kinfolk: our poetry, prayers, and memories of our childhood as cousins sharing a common spiritual heritage.

One of the most cherished things you can give your children and grandchildren is a written record of your troubles and failures, joys and successes as a Christian. Tell them your story: how God led you through the hard times and how His love prevailed as you lived in it during your struggles. Tell them how He held you up during the chaotic times, keeping your mind on Him. Give them suggestions on how to pray, how to live a Christian life, and how to keep a steady Christian focus on the face of Christ, regardless of circumstances.

Today I received a letter from Earl containing a fascinating writing about his childhood: of the bully in his neighborhood, of wearing knickers to school, of hauling buckets of coal for his mother to a rented upstairs apartment, of riding in his friend Mutt's big open-top Franklin automobile, and of winning the fourth grade championship title in an exciting marble tournament. On the cover he printed:

Every man's work, whether it be literature or music or pictures or anything else, is always a portrait of himself, and the more he tries to conceal himself the more clearly and the more he tries to conceal himself the more clearly
—Samuel Butler (1835-1902)

Write truths you'd like to pass along, as Earl is doing, to another generation.

_____

_____

_____

_____

For Inspiration

Written prayers inspire. Hundreds of books have been sold containing pages of prayers of famous and not-so-famous people. Think of someone whose prayers have inspired you. I grew up on the prayers of Peter Marshall and Billy Graham, which have changed my life. Other prayers I read have affected me in similar ways, though the pray-ers were not famous clergy, but ordinary Christians. Don't deny your Christian friends inspiration by failing to write your prayers. Share your prayers with others you know, especially those who don't go to church anywhere. Include in your prayer journal: Scriptures about Jesus and salvation, cutout pictures of missionaries or others for whom you're praying, church bulletins or newsletters with information about prayer or prayer poetry, scrapbooking borders or decorations to make the journal attractive, or special prayers written in calligraphy or other beautifully illustrated letters. You may, like many Christians who enjoy journaling, keep a private journal for intimacy with God, and a public journal for sharing with others, when appropriate. You can be a blessing to others by sharing your prayer journal with them. Dare to share inspiration.

Write a sentence or two that you've learned in your lifetime that may contain inspiration for others.

_____

_____

_____

_____

M & M: Ministry and Missions Moment

Dear Christian sister, when you're troubled or experiencing a trial, your witness has more value and validity because you've lived through the dark valley. No one can take away from you the lessons you learned through hard times. Share those through a prayer journal. Start by journaling your prayers just for this week.

—— Study 25 ——

Worldwide Prayer Chains

"Celebrating Easter is exciting in Central and Eastern Europe. Christians exchange text messages proclaiming 'Jesus is risen,' replying: 'He is risen, indeed!'" says Mark Sauter, sharing his excitement of this day with those on the other side of the ocean. Mark says, "What great joy it is for us to serve the risen Savior! We've celebrated by email this morning in the Czech Republic, Slovakia, Hungary, Romania, Poland, and Moldova. Our heart and passion has been to continue having that opportunity." Mark's wife Vesta's parents were deaf, and God was able to use her experience with them to minister to hearing-impaired people in hundreds of places. When Mark emailed these words, there was doubt they could return to their work with deaf people in Europe.

January 2006 was a special celebration for Mark and his wife Vesta. Two years before, she had developed a brain tumor (see the story in Study 10). Doctors discovered three suspicious spots. She had brain surgery in Hungary, and in January 2006, the doctors declared her well enough to return to Europe. Mark says, "We have been reminded daily of the words of the psalmist: 'to declare your lovingkindness in the morning, and your faithfulness every night' (Psalm 92:2 NKJV). Some of the days have been long and anxious for us, but His lovingkindness and faithfulness, for which we gave thanks morning, noon, and night, never waned! We were reminded of Peter's encouragement regarding suffering: 'Let those who suffer according to the will of God commit their souls to him in doing good, as to a faithful Creator' (1 Peter 4:19 NKJV). The heavenly Father has been faithful every step of this journey."

Another missionary couple, Mike and Sue, had been on several mission trips, and finally were appointed as missionary associates to a Eurasian country. As soon as they arrived, Sue became very sick with asthma. They say, "Prayers were sent our way by the tons, from not only our church and family, but from churches and people all over the globe. How Amy's updates (their daughter) reached so many people, cities, states, and even countries is amazing. Only God could have taken her updates and spread them from email to hand like a blazing fire. We received hundreds of get-well messages from kindhearted folks who would start off by saying, "You do not know me, but I just wanted you to know I am praying diligently for your fast recovery." That was typical of the deluge of mail that reached us—warming our hearts and encouraging us daily. It is solely due to the faithful intercession of our prayer warriors and the Lord's healing powers that I am now resting at a guesthouse in a large city. We hope to return to our village later, if all plans fall into place."

At Home Anywhere

One characteristic of mature Christians is that they are relaxed and at home wherever they live—whatever the trouble, whatever the setting. This principle is especially true of missionaries. Paul, a first-century missionary, says, "I have learned to be content whatever the circumstances."

Jacob's son Joseph was a young man with great self-esteem. After he had received dreams from God of his being a leader of the rest of the family, he shared them with his brothers, who were jealous.

Read Genesis 37:2-11 and list evidence you see of Joseph's self-esteem.

_____

_____

_____

_____

Joseph's father's love gave him great self-esteem, as our Heavenly Father's love does. His ornate coat, a physical gift from his father, was a sign of his father's love, just as the spiritual gifts you have signify your Father's love. Joseph dared to share dreams that caused more jealousy and hatred from his brothers. Sometimes when you share your hopes and dreams, you may see jealousy or hatred in the eyes of your human sisters and brothers (co-workers, neighbors, friends). However, Joseph remained steadfast.

Read Genesis 37:12–28, and list the two stages of Joseph's troubles.

1. _____

_____

2. _____

_____

At Home in a Dry Place

Like you, Joseph seemed to be innocently minding his own business, being obedient to his father, when his brothers threw him into a pit. Have you ever been in a dry place? Every mature Christian can remember times of spiritual dryness. God sends those times (or allows them to occur in our lives) to refine us. _Joseph's first stage_ *of spiritual growth was probably realized in that cistern.* There, in the shadows of a deep pit, he changed from being a shameless tattletale (Genesis 37:2) to a confident man of faith who could feel at home anywhere, as long as he had faith in God. God leads you to be "in Him" (John 14:10–12), a state that brings contentment, no matter where you are.

During the dry times, God polishes you so your heart is ready to take the next step: moving to a worldwide focus. Just as God moved Joseph from the first stage, a dry pit, to the second stage, a worldwide adventure, He will move you. God always moves maturing Christians from a narrow focus on Him to an wide-open focus on the world.

Read Genesis 39:1–5, and list signs that God was moving Joseph from a local focus in a dry place to a wider, world focus in a place of influence.

_____

_____

_____

_____

_____

_____

Widening Your Focus

Through the Ishmaelite slave traders who bought Joseph from his older brothers, God moved him from a dry place of little influence to a wide place of worldwide influence. Egypt, hundreds of miles away from Canaan, was light years away in culture and wealth.

Joseph rose to the top immediately. Potiphar, an influential official of Pharoah, took Joseph right to the top. Joseph blessed Potiphar and his household (Genesis 39:5). A key to his success is found in verse 2: "The Lord was with Joseph." In other words, Joseph had God in his heart, and God was *in him*, enabling Joseph to be at home anywhere, with faith to thrive confidently.

Because of Joseph's handsome appearance, Potiphar's wife flirted with him; he spurned her advances, and she had him placed in prison under false accusations (Genesis 39:6b–23). However, God's Word says, "While Joseph was there in the prison, the Lord was *with him*" (verses 20–21), giving him a wider and wider focus, even when—again—he was in a dry place.

One important phrase introduces this last segment of Joseph's maturation: "Some time later" (Genesis 40:1). You may wonder what Joseph's thoughts were during those days in prison. Did he whine or wail that God hadn't delivered him? Did he get discouraged, in a strange land with no family to support him? Scripture tells us he made the best of the time, networking with others, making order out of chaos there in the jail. Although he had been enslaved and imprisoned unfairly (Genesis 40:15), he worked as hard as he could, trying to influence others for good instead of evil.

Other words move time forward. "After they had been in custody for some time" (Genesis 40:4); "When two full years had passed" (Genesis 41:1). After Joseph was forgotten, he must have experienced some down times (Genesis 40:23). No matter how many dry places he lived through, Joseph trusted God to take him to the next level of influence. Your job—and that of all Christians—is to trust God, to live in Him and with Him so that our faith sustains us to be other-centered, ministry-centered believers with an evangelical worldview.

Later God moved Joseph from prison to the throne room to rule Egypt, second only to Pharoah (Genesis 41:41). Joseph moved out!

He traveled all over the Egyptian empire (Genesis 41:46). Through His assessment and wise planning, with God's help, he saved not only the Egyptians but his own Hebrew people from starvation and famine (Genesis 40:6 to 47:27).

Widening Your Prayers

As Joseph widened his influence, you can widen yours. Even if you have little physical ability to travel or limited jurisdiction over others, you can use the powerful tool of prayer to show you care for the world. Sue and Mike say, "Christian people not only sin against the unsaved in every land, but against Jehovah Himself when they fail to pray for the redemption of humanity for whom Christ died." You can be a part of God's network today as you never could before. The Internet is filled with prayer requests from all over the world. You're no longer limited to your own experience. Besides, prayer is an open avenue to the world. It transcends time and space, allowing you to move the distance of the universe, to make an impact on faraway affairs as well as situations at your own doorstep. Retired missionary Indy Whitten says in her book *Sent to Love*: "Through prayer you take love's magic carpet to everywhere." As you pray for others, you forget about your own troubles. You also recognize the truth: you have cause for praise when you see others in worse condition than you.

One of the avenues Christians use to share prayer concerns is a prayer chain, as mentioned in Study 22. One person calls another, who calls another, who calls another, until the last person on the chain calls the first person to let her know the circle is complete. Sometimes Christians employ a prayer pyramid, in which the person who hears a prayer request calls three more people, who call three more, who call three more, and so forth. A group of 36 people then call the initiator, who hears the pyramid is complete. Computer-generated email has exploded the prayer chain/pyramid idea. Its effectiveness has exponentially enlarged the number of contacts in every direction. Every day I receive unexpected emails from people all over the world. If you know even one or two missionaries, write them and ask for their email address; then you can get daily or weekly prayer requests to touch the world.

Worldwide Influence: Long Thoughts

When the Tsunami left parts of India, Thailand, and Indonesia in shambles with thousands dead, Christians all over the world prayed for them. As a result of God's miracles (and the caring, witnessing Christians who poured in by the planeload to help with disaster relief and recovery), more than 607,000 new believers were baptized. God amazes us when His Spirit moves over the face of the earth, just as He did when He moved over the face of the deep at Creation. Even when a disaster like a tsunami washes over humanity, God uses the tragedy for good.

Your troubles fade as you see the needs of others. Fannie E. S. Heck, a North Carolina woman who inspired many Christian women in prayer and missions, said, "Think long thoughts."

M & M: Ministry and Missions Moment

Only your unwillingness to serve God through a prayer ministry limits your worldwide influence. Start now. The sky's the limit! This week, ask your pastor or missions leader at church to help you contact those who send prayer request lists. Be sure to include the needs in your local church as well as state, national, and worldwide needs. "Think long thoughts."

Unit 6

———— • ————

REJOICING AFTER THE STORM

Glory to God! After the tough times are over, you take a pause and give a sigh of relief. However, you know as long as you live on this earth, troubled times will return. When the storm has passed, you're wiser, growing exponentially in Christian maturity. Now's the time of rejoicing and refreshing.

Share your contagious praise, so that others find deep-down joy, and vicariously benefit from your experience. You can prevent much human misery by sharing what you've learned from your troubled times of life. Shout it out! Whether you choose to praise Him with voice or written words, tell it to the world. Step by step, woman by woman, make a difference as you change depression to joy in others. Don't keep His overcoming power a secret: tell it out; record your religious autobiography. Enjoy the calm after the storm. You're now a God-ready woman.

. . . .

It's over, Lord. You brought me through!
No longer weary, hurt, and sore.
The storm's passed by, and I'll tell others:
Fuller life they can explore.
    Help me praise You—seek your heart,
    I'll rest in You, forevermore!

—ee

. . . .

─── Study 26 ───

Wise Counsel from a God-Ready Woman

Everyone needs counsel at one time or another. I've been fortunate to have churchwomen, Christian parents, and others giving me wise counsel. Informal counselors have helped steer me in the right direction when I followed wrong paths. *The Message* says, "God sticks his head out of heaven. He looks around. He's looking for . . . just one God-ready woman" (Psalm 14:2). *Troubled times make you God-ready.*

Whatever the trial, after it's over you can offer your testimony as wise counsel. You are now God-ready! It takes only one woman to obey God and change your world, alleviating pain, bringing hope. As a Christian, you have God's wise counsel to give you wisdom for your counseling. David said to God, "You hold me by my right hand. You guide me with your counsel" (Psalm 73:23–24).

Most people don't need professional counseling, but they need a listening ear. Without the in-living Christ in their spirits, non-Christians and immature Christians are vulnerable to hurts. They need your counsel, because you've learned from Him. Experienced in tough times, you're particularly well qualified to share how God led you through troubled waters.

Write the name of one person who might need you as a counselor friend now.

Learning from Troubles and Trials

As we've learned in previous chapters, God allows crises to wake you up from your blurred vision that you are perfect. Troubled times teach you to be a better person, worthy of sharing what you have learned with others. You are qualified to give counsel because you have learned that:

1. You are Crafted

You recognize you are crafted by God, your Creator. "For you created my inmost being; you knit me together in my mother's womb. I praise you because I am fearfully and wonderfully made; your works are wonderful, I know that full well" (Psalm 139:13–14). Since God makes no mistakes, you recognize that all things in His creation, including you, are made according to His will. As we've affirmed earlier in this book, you're His workmanship, the work of His hands (Ephesians 2:10).

What a great truth to share! God is the maker of every troubled woman who feels sorry for herself. With care He went through the complicated process of creating her to be unique, and you can teach her that. Though you were saved by grace, not works (Ephesians 2:8–9), the second half of Ephesians 2:10 reads: "created in Christ Jesus to do good works, which God prepared in advance for us to do." Because He created you in just the way you are, He designed you to tell others He created them just they way *they* are, in order to serve Him in their own unique way.

2. You are Confident

You are assured, you are confident in God, your trusted protector. Within the process of moving through chaos and coming out on the other side, you find confidence in Almighty God, the only true source of confidence.

The first winter I spent with a small baby, I struggled with his morning wake-up call: loud crying that I couldn't easily stop. He also had colic every afternoon, and I washed a pail full of diapers daily, hanging them on an outside line where they froze stiff in the cold weather. (Those were the days without upset-stomach drops, disposable diapers, or clothes dryers.) At 22, I felt if I had survived that winter, I could survive anything! I learned confidence based on God's Word and strength through that cold winter. As the years have passed, I've gained more confidence and "hold fast the confidence and the rejoicing of the hope firm to the end" (Hebrews 3:6 NKJV).

As a young woman, which experiences gave you confidence?

_____

_____

_____

_____

_____

How can your share them with others?

_____

_____

_____

_____

3. You are Carried

You acknowledge you've been carried by Him, your eagle's wings. You remember times He carried you when you didn't have the heart to go on. "I love you, God—you make me strong. God is bedrock under my feet, the castle in which I live, my rescuing knight" (Psalm 18: 1–2 The Message). Tell another woman about how many times God must have carried you on His wings and rescued you like a knight in shining armor.

Read Psalm 91:1, 4, 14–15. Write about times you know God must have carried you through.

_____

_____

_____

_____

_____

Thank Him.

4. You are Completed

You have a sense of being completed by Him, your Almighty Creator. Once God created you, then He has constantly been perfecting you (also called sanctifying you, or completing you). New Testament Christians prayed for one another, "that ye may stand perfect and complete in all the will of God" (Colossians 4:12 KJV). When you're being completed by God, as He finishes and redeems His creation, you can witness under His power to help others be complete.

5. You are Counseled

You feel able to offer counsel from Him, your Comforter, because He's given all for you. You're filled with wisdom because you've sat at the feet of the Master and absorbed great understanding and discernment. When asked how he decided to be a counselor, a doctor in our town said, "In my experience, I've studied about counseling, gone to counseling, listened to counseling, had great teachers on counseling, and then practiced counseling. I was 'all counseled up.'"

M & M: Ministry and Missions Moment

You're "all counseled up" if you've read your Bible for years, studied God's Word through Christian materials, and prayed for wisdom. God has led you to overflow with His fullness. "You have been given fullness in Christ" (Colossians 2:10).

Let His wisdom flow through you; remember what He taught you. As a God-ready woman, as God gives opportunity, counsel someone this week.

Study 27

Contagious Praise

One night when I was seven, my father drove us to a nearby town in our old T-Model Ford. My brother and I sat in the back seat half asleep, when I heard a commotion in the front. Raising up (there were no seat belts in those days!) I saw we were driving down a steep hill, and my father was holding the steering wheel in his hand—not connected to the steering column beneath it! Without any way to steer, he was hanging on to what was left of the wires coming out of the steering column while passing the decapitated steering wheel to Mother, whose eyes were wide open with fear! My father stood on the brakes with both feet, finally bringing the car to a halt, just short of falling over a steep bank.

I'll never forget my father's words: "Thank the Lord for good brakes!" Mother, Jim, and I applauded! As an adult, when I think of all the words that could have spewed out at such a time, I'm grateful for a godly father, who praised his Lord in an emergency.

All of us love to hear praise. My father's words enriched our spirits. The next car along took us back about a mile to an uncle's house, and he took us the other ten miles home. We sang on the way, thankful to be alive!

Read Psalm 150:1–6. List ways you can praise God.

_____

_____

_____

_____

Signs of Nature's Praises

Just as God says we are to praise Him with musical instruments, He says the angels, sun, moon, and stars praise Him. The sea creatures praise Him. Lightning, hail, clouds, mountains, trees, animals, and birds praise Him. Kings and all rulers, young and old men, women and children praise Him (Psalm 148-1-12). Trees of the forest will sing for joy at His coming (Psalm 96:12b), and rivers clap their hands (Psalm 98:8). Jesus Himself said, the rocks would cry out if Christians didn't praise God! (Luke 19:40). We look for signs in nature that show His praises.

Physical Signs on the Journey

Kira Trexler from Charlotte, North Carolina, tells the story of her grandfather whom she calls "my hero." He had served in a faraway war, where he experienced hair-raising horrors. Haunted by this experience, he drifted away from his family, finding solace in alcohol and drugs. Kira met him for the first time when she was ten. He told her about the worst experience of the war.

In one skirmish, the enemy ambushed him and his friends. Once the smoke cleared, many were dead and dying all around him. He searched for his best friend, and found him lying in a ditch. He cared for his mortal wounds and waited for help, which came only after his best friend had died. He told Kira with wet eyes that as he held his dying friend in his arms, he started to pray for the first time, for forgiveness and for peace. Not knowing whether or not God had heard him, he looked up to see a beautiful eagle circling overhead. He saw eagles occasionally after that, and thought of

God's faithfulness and strength. Just as he shared with Kira, you may also remember a time of terror when a physical sign reminded you that God is with you always. Physical signs provide a constant reminder—in troubled times or calm—of spiritual truth: God is good. He gives us an inner spiritual inheritance that can never perish.

Signs of Trouble, Signs of Praise

First Peter 1:4, 6–7 says you have "an inheritance that can never perish, spoil or fade—kept in heaven for you. . . . In this you greatly rejoice, though now for a little while you may have had to suffer grief in all kinds of trials. These have come so that your faith—of greater worth than gold, which perishes even though refined by fire—may be proved genuine and may *result in praise*, glory and honor when Jesus Christ is revealed."

Your faith is proved genuine when you obey and work for Jesus, no matter what the sacrifice. Praise Him in the tough times.

Do you have a favorite sign that brings you joy and certainty of the presence of Jesus? If so, write it below. Share with a friend, if appropriate.

_____

_____

_____

_____

Do you have a Scripture verse you read to encourage you in times of trouble? Write it below.

_____

_____

_____

_____

_____

_____

What have you done to share your story of God's physical signs of spiritual faithfulness? You can share a Scripture or other sign with others who may be troubled.

Email Messages as Signs

Jennifer Rothschild, author of *Lessons I Learned in the Dark*, tells in an email message about a day when she was trying to work in a cluttered house. Unable to stand it any longer, she began cleaning out things her husband loved but had left in disarray. She says, "I dragged $3,000 worth of Yamaha, Peavey, and Bose up the basement stairs and heaved them into the back of the truck!" After she'd delivered them to the local Victory Mission, she felt cleansed and able to work in an uncluttered room. Then she remembered God's Word: "This is the one I esteem: he who is humble and contrite in spirit, and trembles at my word" (Isaiah 66:2).

Contemplating her actions, she says, "Unbridled volition screams to the world, 'It's my way or the highway' and 'I'd rather ask forgiveness than permission.' But meekness and a surrendered will always says, 'I will seek permission so I don't have to seek forgiveness.'"

Jennifer obviously has a gift of administration.

She says, "Unbridled volition, a will out of control, invites destruction. Meekness, however, a will bridled and cooperative, experiences an uncluttered, clean heart."

How can you show an attitude of praise rather than an attitude of "unbridled volition," as Jennifer says?

_____

_____

_____

Cyberspace Signs

Ruth Duke, missionary wife in California, wrote *The King's Kid: Overcoming with Multiple Sclerosis*, about her experiences of losing parents at an early age, being adopted by the pastor's family at her church, and continuing to serve God through music and teaching after finding out she had a crippling disease. One day she got a letter in the mail from someone in Texas. A Christian women's book club had reviewed her book and wrote the following comments:

"We were so impressed by your book that we reviewed it in our missions group."

"We admire the way you continue to serve our Lord."

"God bless you and your Christian spirit."

"Praise God for your wonderful life!"

Would you think riding in a wheelchair is a wonderful life? Do you think a life of pain and struggling to walk around from cabinet to cabinet in your own kitchen is a blessing? Ruth sees her life as a blessing. I know she's a blessing to me. Together we, along with two other women, established the Valley Christian Writers Association, which she continued long after the rest of us were gone from her community. She's a woman of tremendous strength who has served God well for many years as a missionary, a leader in her church and state women's work, as well as serving as the wife of a director of missions/ministries for hundreds of Christians in a central California county. Her sweet spirit encourages many people to praise God.

Ruth tells of the book being a blessing to others across the nation. She has had numerous phone calls and email messages from people who have passed *The King's Kid* around. "I have many cyber-friends," Ruth says. One of them shared many books in a prison ministry in Virginia. Through Ruth's book, the cyber-friend encouraged people in jail to keep holding on, no matter what the circumstance. Ruth's daughter, Melissa Wagner, a missionary in Venezuela, was in the United States, staying in Richmond, Virginia (at the International Mission Board), when Ruth (and husband, Jack) visited her there and arranged to meet the cyber-friend for dinner. Together they celebrated what God had done, praising Him for the way He moves in cyberspace as well as in local communities, performing miracles from one place to another!

Ruby Buckley, a suicide survivor of her late son, John David, published *The Heart Binder for the Wounded,* her story of restoration of the broken pieces and comfort she received from God's heart to hers. She says the large jagged-edged pieces become ground into sand—gold sand from God, who wraps them in a bandage so they are hardly noticeable in busy Christian lives of joy and service to God. She shares her vision of John David at peace. She then tells how God showed her a gold hammer and nails to nail down boards of forgiveness in her memories, to build a bridge of love that restored her heart and relationships. Her book has cheered me for years, and I've passed it along to others who need to praise God in tough times.

How can you use cyberspace or pass-around books to help others praise God? Write a few ideas below.

_____

_____

_____

_____

_____

_____

_____

_____

Once upon a time there was a king with a giant vase. Wealthy princes brought great bouquets of expensive flowers that looked beautiful in the vase, but since the vase was vast, it needed more flowers. Finally a little girl brought the most ugly dandelion in the kingdom and slipped it in the side of the vase. Immediately the other flowers shifted, and that flower filled the space, making it the centerpiece for the entire arrangement; a beautiful, frilly yellow ball shining like the sun.

Perhaps you think you have no spectacular story for which to praise God. You often don't think of praise words to share at the right moment. Every woman can praise God in whatever way He gives her, and it will be just the right touch to fill His vase. He takes our words, our stutters, and our humble hearts and makes our praise a thing of beauty.

M & M: *Ministry and Missions Moment*

You may want to use your administrative skills to teach an attitude of gratitude. You can give written words of praise to others to use in their private time with God, or in witnessing to those in need. Whatever you do, give it to God as a beatitude of gratitude.

Jesus said of the woman who worshipped at His feet, "She did what she could" (Mark 14:6). This week, do what you can, where you are, to show contagious praise.

Study 28

Shout It Out! Writing Your Story

I was busy in my office in the Baptist Building in Fresno, California. Every day I drove to San Francisco, flew to San Diego, or phoned a variety of women among the 33 million people all over the state. As I tackled another stack of papers in my inbox that had accumulated while I was out of town, a young woman strode into my room carrying a briefcase. Dressed in a businesslike navy blue suit, this confident baby boomer said, "I'm Tricia Scribner, and I want you to mentor me!"

I was taken aback, not knowing what to say after the abrupt request. I felt as if I were in the post office facing the recruiting poster: "Uncle Sam wants you!" I took a step backwards and asked her to sit and talk a few moments. I explained that, though I might want to mentor her, I was just too busy. My responsibilities already had given me too much on my plate.

As she turned to go, she asked me to lunch. "I'm downtown anyway, and I have to eat—and you have to eat somewhere. Why not go with me?" And then she said the magic words: "My treat!"

Of course I accepted the free lunch. We ate a chicken sandwich and talked about why she was seeking a mentor. She had teenagers, a stage of life that I had survived, and we shared things we had in common. Then she revealed her greatest desire: She had prayed for over 15 years for a writing mentor. No one had accepted her invitation, though she had asked several good prospects to mentor her.

For weeks Tricia and I had lunch together (her treat). After six weeks I realized I was mentoring her. We talked about parenting and the basics of writing. Knowing that I didn't want to mentor her, I decided I'd sharpen her writing skills with the difference between *who* and *whom*, one of the hardest grammar problems, thinking that puzzle would discourage her from writing. How I underestimated Tricia's perseverance and intelligence! She studied the pronouns for weeks. One day she called and said, "Edna, I'm tired of *who* and *whom*. I've reached the point where I say, "Whom cares, anyway?" We laughed and then she explained one sentence that had really caused her concern. I realized at that point that she was showing much progress in her grammar understanding. She soared! A few months later, she even corrected my usage of *who* and *whom*. As our mentoring relationship grew, I realized I had more to offer than I had previously thought. Tricia and I began a writing partnership that continues today. I've realized that mentoring is sometimes a lifetime commitment.

However, God has taught me much more about my life through the persistence of this young woman. I now know that many women my age won't mentor because they feel they have nothing to offer. I've talked to hundreds of them and I find this common denominator in most Christian women. However, they do rise to the challenge when they see the needs of spiritually younger women. Many of them feel called to a special place of service in the mentoring arena. God has given each of them a passion for one certain thing: French cooking; parenting; witnessing; prayer; gardening; scrapbooking; computer records management; car mechanics; or a great number of other things.

God has called me to mentor other people in their writing. I am now mentoring nine young women by email, two women in my church, and many others at writers' conferences and women's conferences, where I go as God leads me. God has multiplied my ministry many times. It's amazing to see how God enabled my English teacher as a child and teen to show me what I needed for life, how He implanted into my life what I'd need for an adult ministry years later. Looking back, I can see how "all things work together for good to them that love God, to them who are the called according to his purpose" (Romans 8:28).

God's Hand in Your Life

I still stand in awe that he lifted Tricia from Grayson, Louisiana, and me from South Carolina, and placed us in Fresno, California, for a short period of time so we could meet and form a writing partnership. Each of us benefited from the association. I love her family and she loves mine. I take pride in her husband as he succeeds in life, and her three precious daughters as they grow to adulthood. I'm proud of her latest book, *Unity in Diversity: Rising Above Our Differences* (www.wmustore.com), about how to live in unity with other women's groups in your church. Tricia corrects many of my manuscripts (She especially loves taking a red pen to my *who* and *whom* mistakes!) and I correct her. More importantly, God has enlarged my circle of influence—as well as my lifelong learning—through mentoring. I'm able to reach women writers for Christ, and I learn about Him from them.

How has God given you opportunities in exactly the location where He's placed you?

_____

_____

_____

_____

What kind of skill, spiritual gift, or talent has God given you?

_____

_____

_____

List here things you can do as in a writing or speaking ministry based on what God has given you.

_____

_____

Writing Your Story

If God has blessed you with a message of victory through the tough times of life, you may have a story you would like to write. I suggest to any new writer that you begin with writing small articles for your church. At the very lowest entry point, write a paragraph of practical tips on Christian living for your church newsletter or other local publication. You may write one sentence with a pithy saying to inspire other church members. If you have a county association of churches, they are often looking for fillers in their newsletters. Give them a visit. Volunteer to help fold letters and stuff envelopes, or do other extra jobs in their office. Assess their writing needs and volunteer to help.

You also may find in your local newspaper a welcomed opportunity for publishing your writing. God sends Christian writers to make an influence on their secular world. Most community newspapers have a religion section, where you'll have an entry point into the publishing world. Some successful writers tell about getting their start writing letters to the editor in their city paper. Send a short, informative manuscript to the editor and offer to do follow-up articles.

Use your passion to write a syndicated column. One of my good friends started a small column about mountain folk tales, which he sold all over the country. In it he always included a religious example that pointed to Christ. (He wrote 26 columns at a time and provided the newspapers a six-month supply of weekly articles at once.) He modified his content slightly for the Ozarks, Blue Ridge, Sierra, and Rocky Mountains. Another Christian friend publishes a cooking column offering recipes in a state denominational paper, and a third writes an "around the town" column that always includes local church news for a local newspaper.

Look back at the skills, spiritual gifts, or talents you listed earlier in this chapter. Decide on a passion God has given you in one of these areas. Then write a pithy saying, poem, or small article based on what you know about this area. Make some notes here.

_____

_____

Use Several Kinds of Media

Besides newspapers, magazines are also fertile ground for your writing. You have as much chance as other freelance writers to get an article published. Your Christian message may enrich the article and make it attractive. Get a good guide, such as *The Writers' Market* or *The Christian Writer's Market*, available at bookstores and libraries, to find out what kind of articles magazines accept. Start within your own denomination. Every Sunday School class for adults, youth, children, and preschoolers needs curriculum. Explore what's available in your own church. You can change the lives of many people through your God-given talent in writing. When I was a little girl, I read the biography of James Fennimore Cooper, who was reading a story and complaining to his wife about its quality. He said, "I could write better than this!" His wife challenged him to write a better one, and he did, finishing *The Last of the Mohicans* and several other books. If you are now reading this book, and thinking "I could do better than this," then do it! Write a Christian book.

After beginning with many, many articles, you will more easily make a transition to books.

Network with Writers and Editors

Networking is extremely important. Ask where critique groups for writers meet in your area. Attend as a guest at their meetings, and ask to join. Go to every writers conference you can afford. You'll find them in every state, every season. I've belonged to a writer's critique group in three towns, two of which I had to begin myself, even long before I'd published the first small article. I still keep in touch with many of the members of those groups, some of whom have published wonderful books. Occasionally I'll get an auto-graphed book in the mail, with a thank you note from the proud author. When you have spreading the gospel as a common goal, you'll find your friendships eternal.

M & M: *Ministry and Missions Moment*

Christians need to be in the communications business. As you meet networking groups, you will find witnessing opportunities. Most writers also learn to be speakers, to get their God-given message to more people who need His love. Begin by speaking in your church or women's group.

You will never know whether your work will be successful until you try. Pray, asking God to lead you; then decide *exactly* what your passion is. Focus on following His leadership in whatever way He wants to use your God-given yearnings to serve Him through His special touch in your life.

—— Study 29 ——

Sharing Your Spiritual Autobiography

If you don't want to be a writer, what do you do with your story? Everyone has a story to tell about their adventures in life. God dazzles us with the excitement of the journey as we go deeper and deeper still into His mind and Spirit. Sharing that excitement is one of the most beneficial disciplines of life. One suggestion for a person of any spiritual maturity is to write your spiritual autobiography.

Your purpose in writing a spiritual autobiography is twofold: (1) self-discovery as you arrive at a new understanding of who you are as an in-living Christian, and (2) spiritual growth as you increase your awareness of God and what He's doing in your life.

You don't have to complete this autobiography now, but you should fill in a few lines as an outline of what you will write later. I suggest you write, not in this outline form, but in paragraphs with general headings and subheadings. Purchase a beautiful journal or writing tablet to write your autobiography, or type it at the computer and print it on beautiful papers. Put thought into each part, and it will last as a witness to the goodness of God—through good times and bad—from generation to generation.

My Spiritual Autobiography

1. Early Years

A. Describe your life as a child.

- Where you were born/extraordinary circumstances of your birth, if any:
- Your parents:
- Special qualities of your parents:
- Your grandparents:
- Special qualities of your grandparents or other extended family:
- Your cultural heritage (race, language, dialect, differences among and outside the family, history of extended family's journey—how they got to the place where you were born):
- Siblings, including birth order and characteristics:
- Others who lived in the home:
- Your role in the family:
- Specifics about how you related to your parents and brothers and sisters:
- Special events in early childhood:

B. Describe your religious training as a child.

- Special religious meaning to your birth, if any:
- The religious practices of your family (family devotions, private devotions, church attendance, Bible study, prayer practices):
- The impact of your church, friends, and community on your religious life:

C. Describe your conversion experience (move this item to later in life if this did not happen early in life).
- What your conversion meant to you at the time/at the present time:
- Factors and persons influential in your decision and experience:

D. Describe your evaluation/appreciation for your early religious training and experiences as you have grown older and matured.
- Your acceptance of what you were taught:
- Your reaction/modification of previous beliefs or practices:
- The effect your previous training has on you now:

2. Years of Spiritual Pilgrimage
A. Describe the high points and low points of your spiritual pilgrimage.
- Periods of uncomplicated, exuberant joy in Christ:
- Doubts and challenges to your faith:
- Persons who influenced you:
- Significant events with a religious impact on you:
- Significant commitments (missionary, clergy, etc.):
- Reasons you changed affiliation of church or denomination, if applicable:
- Effects of advanced education and/wider cultural exposure on your spiritual maturation:
- Results of any horizontal mobility (geographical movement) on your religious growth:
- Results of any vertical mobility (change in social/economic class) on your growth:
- Effects of illnesses, tragedies, deaths on your religious understanding:

B. Describe your present spiritual condition.
- How you feel toward God:
- How you believe God feels toward you:
- Your attitude at this time toward religious practices (church attendance, family devotions, private devotional life, etc.):
- Sources of religious education and growth now:
- Special insights:

C. Describe in detail how you have recognized God's action in your life.
- The process of how you have come to an understanding of God's will for you:
- The history of your adult prayer life:
- How you've grown in your understanding of prayer:
- The differences God's in-living (or indwelling Spirit) makes in your marriage, if applicable:
- The differences His in-living has made as a parent, if applicable:
- The differences His in-living has made in your work:
- The differences His in-living has made in your acquisition/ use of material possessions:
- The differences His in-living has made in your recreation:
- The differences His in-living has made in your friends/ other relationships:

3. Future Years

A. Describe your goals for fulfillment in life.
- How your spirituality and religion affect these goals:
- Where you're headed in your spiritual pilgrimage:

B. Describe your feelings about death.
- Your assurance about death:
- Your challenges about facing death:
- Your feelings about life after death:
- Scriptures of hope and assurance:

C. Other (life Scripture/mantra, mission statement, spiritual philosophy, etc.).

After preparing your spiritual autobiography, share it with a group of other Christians or interested persons who want to reflect on their spiritual pilgrimage. Specify how you recognize God at work in you and what a difference it makes. Speak only of your own experiences; don't try to tell them theirs.

When you've shared, give others the opportunity to ask questions, request any clarification they need, or make comments. Give them time to consider the implications of your observations about your walk with God. They will see similarities and differences in how people view, interpret, and/or describe the actions of God in their lives.

Spiritual Autobiography Group Sharing

If all the group wants to share their spiritual autobiographies, give instructions far ahead so each one will have time to prepare his or her autobiography, choose a church or a home in which to meet, and agree on a time.

Give these prerequisites: each person must: (1) share with honesty and integrity, taking the risk of being vulnerable to the group; (2) be open about your deepest concerns in your inner self; (3) have equal responsibility; (4) help create a setting of respect and trust; (5) accept each person's story as valid; (6) avoid trying to prove anything; (7) not interrupt others with a self-centered agenda; and (8) keep shared experiences confidential, if appropriate.

Benefits of Group Sharing

Group sharing of completed spiritual autobiographies provides these benefits:

1. Discovering more about yourself
2. Realizing who you are spiritually
3. Recognizing the influence of others on your life
4. Strengthening your religious convictions and helping others to do the same
5. Gaining confidence in your ability to communicate your faith
6. Enriching the Christian community around you
7. Knowing one another better; bonding in the group
8. Finding a certain measure of catharsis/healing from trauma during troubled times
9. Following the New Testament pattern of Christian witnessing and moral support
10. Recognizing the personal nature of your witness is the source of its persuasive power
11. Comprehending and integrating life events with our culture and religion
12. Understanding Christian conversion is not stereotyped; each experience is unique
13. Discovering the everyday Christian experience is a rich diversity of experience
14. Knowing without a doubt we have much to give one another/ can learn from one another

M & M: Ministry and Missions Moment

This week, fill out your spiritual autobiography. Encourage a group to fill out their spiritual autobiographies. May God bless you as you share your spiritual autobiography with others.

Study 30

The Calm After the Storm

In this book you've taken a realistic look at the pitfalls of life and looked at several approaches to the problem of suffering. You've studied characteristics of a maturing Christian and explored ways you could handle the hurts of life during troubled days. You've been given tools to use for spiritual strength and suggestions for in-living, keeping a peaceful inner spirit in spite of storms in your external environment. In addition, you've looked at ways to find power in His Word, be healed through prayer, and share what you've learned in your darkest hours with other hurting persons. As we've progressed through this last unit, we've considered how to rejoice at the end of a period of crisis and celebrate God's goodness as you face the calm after the storm.

Cherie Nettles (cpnettles@earthlink.net), a vibrant Christian comedienne, says, "First there was my teenage diagnosis with rheumatoid arthritis, my many months in a wheelchair, and the doctor's prediction that I'd never walk again. Then my sister's bitter divorce, the deaths of beloved family members and friends, my mother's failing health, and my ovarian cancer. I could have become bitter, but then the eyes of my heart began to remember just how much God has allowed me to drink from the wellspring of life. I saw my two beautiful children, my wonderful husband, my precious church, my loving family and friends. . . . The fountain is flowing. It is deep, it is wide, so kick off your shoes, roll up your pants, and jump in!"

Cherrie is a person whom I admire. She's experienced much more pain than most people. She has learned to rejoice in the calm after the storm. She's the most exuberant Christian comedienne I know. Jesus said, "Come unto me, all ye that labor and are heavy laden, and I will give you rest" (Matthew 11:28 KJV).

Think of God's Power

Paul said to the Christians at Ephesus: "Now to him who is able to do immeasurably more than all that we ask or imagine, according to his power that is at work within us, to him be glory in the church and in Christ Jesus throughout all generations, for ever and ever! Amen" (Ephesians 3:20–28). The last study of this book is not an end, but a beginning—for you and your family—as you live the stronger-still life. You'll depend on God's abundant power and His faithfulness to stand by you in whatever tough times you face. Praise Him who is Sovereign Ruler, Master of all, and Lord of your life!

My Aunt Alice died today, very quietly taking her last breath. Her legacy will live on for years. I loved her when I was 5 and she was a beautiful 16-year-old. My children loved her because her house was their home-away-from-home, a place filled with her kindness and love. The celebration of her family has been joyous. We have laughed at memories and enjoyed the fellowship with cousins whom we haven't seen for a while. What a great joy to experience a faithful Christian's home-going! She knew how to handle the tough times of life: by in-living, which gave her absolute trust in God to the end.

Keep Your Eyes on Jesus

As you end your studies in this book, face the future with God's blessings. My prayer is that you'll keep your eyes on Jesus as you contemplate His power to overcome the world. I pray that you will accept His in-living in your heart and share your faithful trust with future generations. Be assured God cares about you and has an answer for every dilemma, a comfort for every trauma.

In his book *Knowing God*, J. I. Packer says, "There is, in contemplating Christ, a balm for every wound; in musing on the Father, there is a quietus for every grief; in the influence of the Holy Ghost, there is a balsam for every sore. Would you lose your sorrow? Would you drown your cares? Then go, plunge yourself in the Godhead's deepest sea; be lost in his immensity; and you shall come forth as from a couch of rest, refreshed and invigorated."

M & M: Ministry and Missions Moment

Share with someone this week several truths you learned in this book. Ponder what God has taught you, and find rest in your spirit. As you face the future with hope and faith, dive deeper and deeper still into His Spirit—and as you move ever closer to Him, remember: God says, "This is the resting place" (Isaiah 28:12).

Suggested Reading List

This list is made up of my recommendations for readers who want to pursue further reading as a supplement to your regular Bible study, for help when facing tough times, and for use with support ministries. These books have been reliable helpers for many Christians and can be recommended to others with confidence!
—Edna

Anonymous. *The Cloud of Unknowing.*

A Kempis, Thomas. *The Imitation of Christ.*

Bainton, Roland H. *Here I Stand: A Life of Martin Luther.*

Baxter, Richard. *The Saints Everlasting Rest.*

Bernard of Clairvaux. *On Loving God.*

Bonhoeffer, Dietrich. *The Cost of Discipleship.*

Brother Lawrence. *The Practice of the Presence of God.*

Bunyan, John. *Grace Abounding.*

Buckley, Ruby. *The Heart Binder for the Wounded.* Prentiss, MS: Gems of Grace Ministry (P. O. Box 1285), 1995.

De Chardin, Teilhard. *The Divine Milieu.*

Delp, Alfred. *Prison Meditations.*

Duke, Ruth. *The King's Kid: Overcoming with Multiple Sclerosis,* Rosewood Publishing, 6315 North 8th Street, Fresno, CA93710, (rd2d@sbcglobal.net) 1998.

Eckhart, Meister. *Works.*

Fenelon, Francois. *Christian Perfection.*

Foster, Richard J. *Celebration of Discipline: The Path to Spiritual Growth.*

Fox, George. *Journal.*

Hammarskjold, Dag. *Markings.*

Hinson, Glenn E. *Seekers after Mature Faith.*

Jones, Rufus. *The Flowering of Mysticism.*

Kelly, Thomas. *A Testament of Devotion.*

Kierkegaard, Søren. *Purity of Heart.*

Kok, Elsa. *A Woman Who Hurts, a God Who Heals.* Birmingham: New Hope, 2005.

Ladun, Brenda. *Getting Better, Not Bitter: A Spiritual Prescription for Breast Cancer.* Birmingham: New Hope, 2002.

Law, William D. *A Serious Call to a Devout and Holy Life.*

Leech, Kenneth. *True Prayer: An Invitation to Christian Spirituality.*

Littauer, Florence. *Silver Linings: Breaking Through the Clouds of Depression.* Birmingham: New Hope, 2004.

McCasland, David. *Oswald Chambers: Abandoned to God.* Nashville: Discovery House, 1993.

Merton, Thomas. *The Seven Storey Mountain.*

Nee, Watchman. *The Release of the Spirit.* Richmond: Christian Fellowship Publishers, 1965.

Packer, J. I. *Knowing God.* Downer's Grove, IL: InterVarsity Press, 1993.

Sandin, Fran Caffey. *See You Later Jeffrey.* Wheaton: Tyndale House Publishers, 1999.

Scribner, Tricia. *Unity in Diversity: Rising Above Our Differences.* Birmingham, New Hope, 2005.

Sowell, Kimberly, *Journey to Confidence: Becoming Women Who Witness.* Birmingham: New Hope, 2005.

Stewart, Donald. *Refuge: a Pathway Out of Domestic Violence and Abuse.* Birmingham: New Hope, 2004.

Wiersbe, Warren. *Be Mature.* Wheaton: Victor Books, 1978.

Yancey, Philip. *Where Is God When It Hurts?* Grand Rapids: Zondervan, 1977.

New Hope® Publishers is a division of WMU®, an international organization that challenges Christian believers to understand and be radically involved in God's mission. For more information about WMU, go to www.wmu.com. More information about New Hope books may be found at www.newhopepublishers.com. New Hope books may be purchased at your local bookstore.

Other Studies with *Edna*

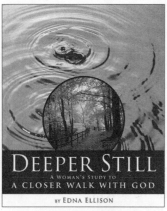

Deeper Still
*A Woman's Study to
a Closer Walk with God*
ISBN-13: 978-1-59669-013-4

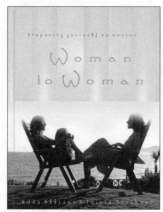

Woman to Woman
Preparing Yourself to Mentor
Edna Ellison and Tricia Scribner
ISBN-10: 1-56309-949-7

Friend to Friend
*Enriching Friendships Through
a Shared Study of Philippians*
ISBN-10: 1-56309-710-9

Friendships of Faith
A Shared Study of Hebrews
ISBN-10: 1-56309-762-1

Friendships of Purpose
A Shared Study of Ephesians
ISBN-10: 1-56309-901-2

Available in bookstores everywhere

For information about these books
or any New Hope product, visit
www.newhopepublishers.com.